Dark Starlight Publications Presents

Healing Rains- Keeper of lost Souls Series

By

Patricia Sassy Angel Chiappa

Dark Starlight Publications

2605 Legend Ct

Leesburg, FL 34748

Ordering Information:

Quantity sales. Special discounts are available on quantity purchases by corporations, associations, and others. For details, contact the publisher at the address above.

Orders by U.S. trade bookstores and wholesalers. Contact: Soulbabylondon@gmail.com

Printed in the United States of America 2016

There is a major crisis in this country. Many people with mental illness are not getting the help they need. My mother worked with the mentally ill for many years. She has seen many state hospitals closed, nursing homes and other housing places that help those with mental illness disappear . State budgets have been cut, families don't know where to find help for their loved ones. People who have mental illness end up living on the street with no support, no love, and no care. Many of these poor people end up committing horrible crimes because they are not on proper medication or have no family to help them. Mental illnesses are disorders that affect a person's mood, thoughts or behaviors. Serious mental illnesses include a variety of diseases including schizophrenia, bipolar disorder, panic disorder, obsessive-compulsive disorder and major depressive disorder. Although they can be scary, it is important to remember that these disorders are treatable. Individuals diagnosed with these diseases can live full, rewarding lives, especially if they seek treatment as needed.

Being diagnosed with a serious mental illness can be a shock — both for the person diagnosed and for his or her family and friends. On the other hand, finally obtaining a diagnosis and treatment plan can sometimes help relieve stress in the family and start moving recovery forward. Family members can be an invaluable resource for individuals dealing with serious mental illnesses. By learning more about the illness, you can support your loved one through diagnosis and beyond. Encouraging a loved one to seek help.

While symptoms of serious mental illnesses vary, the following signs are among the more common:

Social withdrawal.

Difficulty functioning at school or work.

Problems with memory and thinking.

Feeling disconnected from reality.

Changes in sleeping, eating and hygiene habits.

Alcohol or drug abuse.

Extreme mood changes.

Thoughts of suicide.

If you're concerned a friend or family member is exhibiting these signs, try to stay calm. It's easy to imagine the worst-case scenario, but signs of mental illness often overlap with other problems. Consider whether there are other circumstances that might be affecting the person's mood or behavior. Did the person recently experience a shock, such as the death of a loved one? Have they recently lost a job or started a new school?

Regardless of your answers to those questions, don't let your fear of a diagnosis prevent you from encouraging your loved one to seek help. Start by talking to him or her. Express your concerns without using alarmist language or placing blame. You might say, "I've noticed that you seem more stressed than usual," or "I've noticed you don't seem like yourself lately." Then back up those statements with facts, pointing out changes in hygiene or daily activities, for example.

Encourage your loved one to talk to a trusted health care provider. If he or she is hesitant to see a mental health specialist such as a psychologist, suggest a visit to a general physician. Offer to accompany them to the appointment if they'd like.

If your family member doesn't take you up on your offer, consider alerting his or her physician's office with your concerns. Though the physician may not be able to share information with you due to privacy laws, it will give the doctor a head's up to be on the lookout for signs of mental health problems.

If you feel your loved one is in danger of harming himself or herself, or harming someone else, that's an emergency. Don't hesitate to call 911. If possible, ask for an officer trained in crisis intervention — many communities have officers on staff who are trained to diffuse a mental health crisis in the best possible way.

It's entirely normal to experience a flurry of emotions when a loved one is diagnosed with a serious mental illness. Guilt, shame, disbelief, fear, anger and grief are all common reactions. Acceptance can take time, both for the diagnosed individual, for you and for other family members and friends. That acceptance happens at a different pace for everyone. Be patient with yourself and others.

One of the most important things you can do to support a family member with serious mental illness is to educate yourself. The more you learn about what to expect, the easier it will be to provide the right kind of support and assistance.

Familiarize yourself with the symptoms of the disease so that you are able to recognize when your family member might be showing signs that his or her illness is not well controlled. Remember, too, that there's a lot of information on the Internet. Some of it is accurate. Some is wildly incorrect. Find trusted sources of information, and don't believe every horror story.

Medications can be helpful for controlling symptoms of many serious mental illnesses. But they might take a while to become effective, and medication alone is often not enough to keep these diseases in check. Encourage your loved one to take advantage of other resources, such as peer support groups and individual and/or group psychotherapy such as cognitive behavioral therapy or social-skills training.

When a loved one is living with serious mental illness, it's easy to want to take charge. That's often especially true when the person is your own child or partner. But taking on complete responsibility for him or her isn't healthy for either of you. Individuals with serious mental illnesses are more likely to thrive when they are allowed to take appropriate responsibility for their own lives. Instead of driving your loved one to every appointment or errand, for instance, help him or her get a bus pass and learn the routes. Rather than preparing every meal for your loved one, teach him or her how to cook some simple, healthy meals.

Individuals with mental illnesses still have an identity, and they still have a voice. Engage your loved one in open and honest conversations. Ask what they're feeling, what they're struggling with and what they'd like from you. Work together to set realistic expectations and plan the steps for meeting those expectations. Recognize and praise your loved one's strengths and progress. Research shows that compared to offering positive support, repeatedly prompting or nagging people with serious mental illnesses to make behavior changes actually results in worse outcomes.

Unfortunately, people living with serious mental illness still experience stigma and misconceptions. While that can be a difficult reality, the fact is that people diagnosed today can expect better outcomes than ever before. Medications have improved, and new evidence-based psychotherapeutic interventions can have powerful and positive effects. So try to stay positive. One of the most important things you can do to support a loved one with serious mental illness is to have hope. Also please report any signs of violence to the police. Mental illness is not always a common thread in all mass shootings. But if history is any indication, the shooter most likely has a history of severe mental health issues that have either gone untreated or undiagnosed. Even though violence overall has been trending downward in the U.S., the roll-call of carnage caused by mass shootings continues to escalate. Over the last three decades, the overall national homicide rate has fallen from 10 per 100,000 in 1980 to 4 per 100,000 today, but the number of mass shootings has risen from 4 per year, between 1900 and 1970, to 29 per year since then.

This rise correlates directly with the closure of the mental health institutions in 1969, according to mental health experts. After they were shuttered, they were supposed to be replaced by community outreach programs. But many of these programs never took root. This story is not based on any recent events, not are any of the characters real. This story was written to shed light on those dealing with Mental illness and the lack of help they receive in this country. People with Mental illness are not monsters, they are our sons, daughters, mothers, fathers, brothers and sisters. This book is dedicated to all my fans new and old. My wish for you is -May your garden of life be rooted in love. May roses of friendship, kindness and faith choke out the weeds of despair, hate and envy! May the blooms of each memory be filled with happiness, family and blessings! But most of all may you find no thrones among the cobblestones of your soul. For we are here to love one another, for love comes from God. He is the only one that sits on a throne.

"Touched- Chapter One"

Nineteen year old Collage freshman Jimmy Winters nervously stood in front of his English Lit class, clearing his throat.

His favorite professor and substitute father Bruce Martin waited for Jimmy to begin.

Jimmy who suffered with adult acme. Who had low self-esteem was the least popular kid of campus. He was very shy. Jimmy was tall and skinny. If his acne didn't give the others on campus ammunition to pick on him his coke bottle glasses did.

Jimmy softly began to speak when Carlos Hernández, the tough 21 year old on campus and in fact the toughest person

in the town of New Milford , C.T. Said,"
Speak up like a real man chump!"

Carlos was not only the son of the biggest donator to the Collage but the son of Bruce's boss. If he were not Bruce would have had him kicked out of the school a long time ago. "Sit down Carlos. Jimmy, please try to speak up. "Bruce said.

Jimmy's palms became sweaty as he tried to raise his voice. " My dad, Simon Winter was born in a small town in Illinois in the 1960s. My grandma used to tell me my father's birth was a miracle in itself."

Carlos interrupted Jimmy again. "What is so special about a redneck being born in some Hick Town?" He said rudely.

Alice Round harp, one of the prettiest women on campus with her long blond hair, sparkling blue eyes and knock-out figure rolled her eyes. "Why don't you give the nerd a break Carlos?" She said. Carlos was her on again off again boyfriend. All-through she wanted to be friends with Jimmy, peer pressure kept her from doing so.

Lee Roy "Leon" Rivers, Carlos' best friend poked Carlos in the ribs saying," You better listen to the Mrs.!" Carlos laughed hard. He then blew a kiss to Alice.

"Please continue from where you left off Jimmy." Professor Bruce said.

Jimmy stumbled for a moment, trying to find his spot. Finally he started again." My father's birth was a miracle. Because he was born while my grandma was buried under a house, that had fallen victim to a f4 tornado!"

The room was a buzz. Even Carlos looked a little bit interested.

"My Grandma delivered her baby under a heap of twisted metal and a crumbling foundation in the mists of this terrible event because my grandfather had died at her side. For three days after the storm hit my grandma kept her baby and herself alive. My grandma swears to this day that two angels one named Sara and another named Turner kept them alive. Oh did I tell you that my grandma was blind? So my grandma and her baby was alone in the pitch black. My dad, Simon Peter who was named after the Priest that saved them both because he heard my dad's cry lived.

Frances Chung ,a Chinese girl who was adopted by a rich American family said, "I find that hard to believe!"

Jimmy who never argued said," I figured no one would so that's why I brought the newspaper clippings that ran in the paper about it."

Just then the bell rang, and everyone got up to leave. But the professor said," We will pick up where we left off tomorrow. Good job Jumbo."

Jimmy who never learned to take a compliment brushed off the kind words and walked out the door.

As soon as Jimmy reached the lush green lawn, he saw Carlos dealing drugs out of the corner of his eyes. The look Carlos shot him left Jimmy shaken.

Everyone around town knew Carlos was nothing but trouble. They knew Carlos always hid a switchblade in his leather jacket and another in his motorcycle boots.

The first run in Jimmy ever had with Carlos was a terrifying one. It was a crisp autumn day. The leaves on the tall Oak trees had started changing colors. New freshman's on Campus scrambled to find their classes on their first magical day of Collage. Jimmy was no different.

Jimmy's mother Nicole, had tearfully dropped her son off at Collage a few weeks before . She had help Jimmy decorate and set-up his private dorm room. Making sure her only child had all the comforts of home, including a small T.V., microwave and blanket for chilly nights.

After a full day of classes, Jimmy ordered take-out for a local pizza joint and headed to his dorm room to study. To his surprise when he opened the door to his room, Carlos and one of Jimmy's child-hood friends Alice was in bed together!

Carlos jumped out of Jimmy's bed buck naked ,grabbing the switchblade from his boot. He pinned Jimmy against the wall with it saying," If you tell a soul about this you won't live to graduate! I will be using your room when I want to be alone with my lady friend. Do you understand?"

Jimmy so shaken, couldn't talk so he shook his head," Yes."

Since then Carlos has bullied Jimmy. Forcing him to do his homework, write his term papers and to do whatever he wanted him to do.

Jimmy sat alone on a bench eating his boring routine lunch. A peanut butter and jelly sandwich, a root bear soda and a ding dong.

Jimmy watched a baby blue jay on a patch of newly seeded grass peck away at the seeds. Jimmy closed his eyes and wished his life was as simple as that birds. He wished he could fly free without worry. He wished someone could see him.

Day dreaming, he did not hear Alice's voice calling him until she was almost right on top of him.

"Looks like you were a million miles away. I was asking you Jimmy, if you could help me study for my Bio- Chemo class. I really need to ace this test." Alice said.

"Sure, what else am I good for?" Jimmy said downtrodden. Alice said," Yes, I would like you to Tudor me. If you are not busy."

Alice, the woman Jimmy loved. Alice the woman whose hair smelled of coconut and sunshine, whose skin glistened like the summer sun, whose smile could outshine God's stars.

"But I thought you never wanted to see me again?" Jimmy asked confused.

"Well, I figured since we are going to be stuck at this God- awful Collage for four years, that we should learn to be civil to one another. So will you help me or not?" Alice asked.

Alice and Jimmy grew up in the same one horse town. They lived next door to one another. Up until the age of five they did everything together. As kids they even vowed to marry one another someday. Then one day that close friendship went sour. When Alice's mother had accused Jimmy's father of putting the moves on her. Jimmy and Alice were no longer allowed to play together.

As Jimmy got older, he came to realize that Alice's mother was an abusive drug addict. He tried to get her help when he turned 17. After tracking Alice and her mother down to a ghetto, a grimy, crime-ridden apartment building in New Jersey. But she refused. It was then Alice said she never wanted to see Jimmy again.

"Alice, I will help you in any way I can. You know you never have to ask me for anything twice." Jimmy replied.

"Good. At 7am, I will meet you in the Study Hall." Alice replied.

Carlos crept around the corner and jumped out making Jimmy jump five feet into the air.

"You are not hitting on my babe are you?" Carlos asked in a fighting tone.

"No, No sir." Jimmy answered almost weeping his pants. Carlos started laughing then.

"So did the nerd agree to do your work Babe?" Carlos asked wrapping his arms tightly around Alice's waist.

Jimmy noticed how Alice tried to squirm away from him. " I told you Carlos, I want Jimmy to Tudor me not do my work! I am here to learn!"

"Whatever, I would still make the Nerd do it, Cause then we would have more time to fool around!" Carlos laughed, He then felt up Alice right in front of Jimmy.

Jimmy felt sick to his stomach as he could see the pained expression of disgust spread crossed Alice's radiant face.

"You know Carlos, I am just more than a pretty face!" Alice demanded to be respected.

Carlos laughed," I know. You got a pretty butt, a pretty bust and pretty legs also."

Alice stormed off. Carlos went after her.

Jimmy's heart beat overtime as he recalled the last few words his father had spoken to him." One kind deed can change the balance of the entire world. Never underestimate the power of kindness, love and faith. Money can never buy happiness, because happiness can't be found in a wallet. It can only be found in the heart of the truly kind. There is nothing more comforting than the gentle reassurance of GOD AND ANGELS their love for you is endless, a constancy through the ups and downs of life, they are always there, always watching, always guiding, always...

The incredible depth of love, the wisdom, the joy, that I have been able to gift myself, when I take time to connect within, is available to all of us, when we allow, when we listen, when we take time to be...

Wishing you the joy of remembering who you truly are, the beauty of your soul..."

Jimmy could not shake the feeling that his father's spirit was surrounding him in that moment. Without realizing that he was doing it he started talking to his dad outload saying," I miss you dad. I wish I could be more like you. I wish people could see that I am not a Nerd."

Carlos and Lee Roy heard Jimmy talking to himself and said," Look at that Freak!"

Leaving Jimmy feeling more awful and freakish than ever before.

Professor Bruce sat in his tan wing back style chair smoking a pipe and reading a bible. From Acts 2:39, He read: "For the promise is unto you, and to your children, and to all that are afar off, even as many as the Lord our God shall call."

Bruce ran his fingers over that passage over and over again. A tear of joy ran down his weather-beaten face. This passage was the one Bruce presented on a plaque to his wife, the night she told him she was carrying their first child. Just one month before she died at the tender age of 22 of a heart attack along with Bruce's child and their dreams. This was part of Bruce's past he would not reveal to anyone. Bruce's beautiful yet faceless child only living in fabricated memories and dreams. It was a painful time in Bruce's life, yet he rejoiced and found peace in knowing his wife and child were in Heaven.

Jimmy turned off the light in his lonely Dorm room. He snuggled down into the afghan his mother made for Jimmy before she got sick. Before Jimmy's world became darker, colder and cruel.

"God, I don't know if you remember me or not but if you do please send me a friend. Amen." Jimmy prayed.

In the middle of the night sirens blared and lights from police cars flashed all over the campus.

Jimmy ran out of his Dorm room shirtless and shoeless. Standing on a patch of grass along with other students they watched the event unfold.

One student who spoke in a British accent said," What the bloody hell is going on?"

Professor Bruce who came back to the campus to grade some papers because he couldn't sleep, joined Jimmy on the grass. He turned to Jimmy saying," Do you know what is happening?"

Jimmy who was at a loss shrugged his shoulders and replied," I have no idea. I was going to ask you the same thing."

For over an hour the students and Campus staff watched a swat team search dorm rooms, class rooms and cars.

Suddenly an all clear was given for everyone to return inside. Baffled everyone lingered outside to try to find out what had happened. Everyone was shocked to see Frances Chung being lead to a police car wearing handcuffs.

Frances was kicking, screaming, crying and trying to bite the police officers.

In Jimmy's English Lit class, one of the other students had learned that Frances was writing " a play" as she called it about blowing up the Collage. The student had been so disturbed about it he had called the police. The student, who was in fact Carlos first reported it to the Dean. But because it was Carlos, he did not take the threat seriously.

But Frances dorm room reviled that Frances had been serious. Inside her room, Police found maps to the school and books on how to make bombs.

No one really knew Frances had a dark side to her. That she had been mentally ill for years. Or that her own mother put her up for adoption because at the age of six, Frances tried to stab her. No one saw the danger in the bright, bubbly and rich girl expect for Carlos.

Jimmy and mostly everybody on the campus was so shaken by what happened they couldn't sleep that night.

Alice was the most upset. Alice and Frances were pretty close. It shook Alice to the core that one of her friends was in so much pain and so sick.

Alice weep herself to sleep that night. Recalling all the warning signs she had ignored for so long.

Most clearly was the one that happened on the Saturday before this very night. Alice and Frances needed to go Christmas shopping for their families. The woman headed to the Mall together one wintery afternoon.

Frances who had a car, picked Alice up. Snow was falling lightly. The roads were not yet slick or dangerous but Alice was cold enough that her teeth were chattering. So she asked Frances to turn up the heat.

Frances did not respond. She just had a wild- look in her eyes. Frances pressed down on the gas pedal so hard that the car took off like a rocket.

"Slow down Frances, you are going to fast!" Alice yelled.

Frances laughed wildly saying," I wonder if we will die tonight?"

"Slow down Frances, you are scaring me!" Alice begged. Frances slowly eased her car to a slow roll. She then laughed off what she just did by saying," I'm sorry Alice, I just wanted to see if this baby could fly." Frances had just gotten the car the week before.

"Well, don't do that ever again! You really scared me!" Alice as white as a ghost said. The young women then drove to the Mall. All the while Alice was trying to shake off what had just happened.

"Frozen in time- Chapter two"

Carlos was also very disturbed that night. Carlos knew about mental illness and the stigma it carried all too well. Carlos understood how mentally ill people hid their faces in shame, was judged, mistreated and misunderstood. Carlos knew how mental illness could break a family apart, and how the children of the mentally ill were sometimes left to fend for themselves.

Tonight, Carlos relived his own personal nightmare as he watched his classmate get led away by police. It pulled Carlos back into a period of his life he rather forget.

The next day students soberly strolled to their classes. Half in disbelief, half scared out of their wits and the others still in shock. Their quiet little campus had been made into a news media frenzy. There was cameras and news reporters all over. They were interviewing the staff, the students and concerned parents.

Professor Bruce opened up his class day, by doing something that could have cost him his job. He bowed his head and lead those students who wanted to pray into prayer. From Psalms 18.28 he prayed," For thou will light my candle. The Lord, my God will enlighten my darkness." May God deliver us all from this nightmare! Until we learn to sit through the deepest of pain without all of the destructive ways that we numb it, we cannot heal. And until we heal, we cannot really live, cannot really smile. Amen!"

Carlos tried to act tough and cool by saying," Yom! I don't pay $30,000 a year to hear a sermon. So can we wrap up all this preaching and get on with this boring class?"

All-through his words were poisonous, his soul was deeply touched by the prayerful moment.

"O.K. class we left off with Jimmy. Jimmy please take your spot in front of the class." Bruce said.

Jimmy shyly got up. He faced his classmates. His hands once again shaking. "When my dad was two years old, his mother now re-married gave birth to another baby boy weighting only one pound. My uncle Alan was born 5 MThs premature. No one really knows why. When my uncle was born they didn't even know if he was going to live through the night. My uncle had many health issues. My grandma had no choice but to leave my dad home a lot with my step-grandfather while she sat in an I.C.U.unit with my sick uncle.

My step-grandfather became resentful of playing "Mr. Mom." And one night he packed his bags and left. My father was only 3. My grandma came home three hours later to find police surrounding her two-bedroom trailer.

She was arrested for leaving my dad home alone.

My grandma cried out," My baby was not home alone. Oh God, what is happening where is my husband and little boy?"

A male officer who was kind then said," Your little boy is fine. He has been taken to the Dept. of Child Warfare for his own protection."

At the Police Station my tearful grandma was booked for child endangerment and neglect.

Alice interrupted with a very heavy heart." What happened to your grandma, dad and Uncle?"

"Well that night when my grandma got arrested, she tried to explain what had happened, but quite frankly because she was an uneducated woman the cops didn't believe her. With no money my grandma could not hire a lawyer. She had no choice to sign my dad and uncle over to the state. My grandma spent two weeks in jail until her case went to trail. Luckily the judge believed my grandma. She was reunited with her sons. She never saw her second husband again. My dad had a hard time getting readjusted to his home life." Jimmy sneezed then.

Lee Roy asked," What happened then?"

"The truth is my grandma lost everything. Her home, her pride and her joy. Grandma, dad and Uncle Alan moved to a shelter. She went on welfare and had to rely on strangers to take care of her. It was while they were living in a shelter that my dad met his best friend, a young black boy by the name of Frenchie Janson. Frenchie was a year younger then my dad. He was the man that would change my dad's life. Frenchie used to say," Impossibilities vanish when a man and his God confront a mountain." Jimmy stopped when the dismal bell rang. Jimmy then turned to Bruce saying," Shall I save the rest for another day?"

"Class, we will pick this up again in the am. If anyone wants to talk to me after class about what happened last night, I am here for you all." Bruce said.

The class slowly left the class, but Jimmy lingered around as he always did.

"Great job speaking to the class today Jimmy. You even captured the attention of Carlos, I think. "Bruce praised.

"Do you really think Carlos was listening to what I said?" Jimmy asked raising a brow.

"Well, I didn't hear him snoring. That's a big improvement." Bruce made Jimmy crack a smile then. "Excuse me Professor. I need to talk to Jimmy alone please." Alice said.

"Sure." The professor shot Jimmy and 'Oh-La-la' look before leaving the pair alone.

"I am sorry, I was not able to meet you this morning to study. I was with Carlos all night." Alice said apoglically.

"Oh, please spare me the details!" Jimmy waved his hand in disgust.

Alice stood with her hands on her hips." Excuse me? Just exactly are you trying to imply? I am not that kind of gal. As a matter of fact Carlos is not my boyfriend! He is my husband! What greater thing is there for human souls than to feel that they are joined for life - to be with each other in silent unspeakable memories? -- You look at your life, the greatest happiness's are family happiness's. -- don't choose your family. They are God's gift to you, as you are to them." Alice blurred out.

Jimmy blinked hard. "Husband?"

"That's right. He is my husband. Do you have an issues with that?" Alice asked poking a finger into Jimmy's chest.

Jimmy was dumfounded." When? Where? How? But most inporantally why?" Jimmy questioned.

"In spite of what you believe Jimmy, Carlos is a very good man. People just don't look past his hard shell. He is caring, loving and kind. The world tells us the importance of face value. We get caught in the superficial, focus on the surface, measure success by appearances. Angels remind us the importance of faith value. You may not see the results of the prayers for a stranger, the kindness to your neighbor, the respect for the Earth; yet your light makes a difference. Doubt not your loving acts. Live life at faith value. Carlos taught me that! I think the loveliest by far is the one whose gentle heart bears a hundred scars from caring, yet still finds a way to pick up the lamp, one more time, to light the way of love..." Alice said.

Jimmy threw his hands up in defeat." Fine, if you want to ruin your life then so be it. All

I want to know is are we going to study or what?"

"Yeah, sure. Can we make it tomorrow after lunch?" Alice asked.

"That would be ok. But don't be late! I do have a life you know." Jimmy said.

Alice's mean- girl laugh cut through Jimmy's soul and filled it with lonely sadness, not even the woman he loved could see the real Jimmy.

As Alice walked away Jimmy felt a heavy weight on his back.

Carlos broke a promise to himself that he made three years ago. A promise he made when he met beautiful Alice. He was never going to walk or be in a jail again.

But today he was going there to help a classmate in trouble.

Carlos swallowed hard as he looked into the eyes of a warden who hated him.

The warden looked Carlos up and down." Well, Well, Well looks like your here again scumbag!"

The comment made Carlos skin crawl. Remaining calm- Carlos said," Actually I am here to see a friend. Her name is Frances Chung."

"Oh yeah! That's crazy girl that tried to blow up your Collage. Yes, I can see why you would be friends with her. Birds of a feather flock together right? We put her on 24 watch last night. The bitch tried to take her own life." The old grizzly bear of a warden replied. He then picked up the phone in his office , he asked one of the guards to take Carlos there.

Carlos had something he needed to say, even if Frances didn't want to listen.

Frances sat on a cold and metal bench in the holding cell wearing plain grey jumpsuit crying.

Her adopted mother, the hoarder and her abusive father did not even come to see Frances that night. When Frances made her one phone call, they even hung –up on her.

The world viewed Frances parents as gems, caring, loving and giving adults –who gave Frances the world at her feet.

Frances, however knew all of their dirty little and disgusting secrets! Secrets that forced Frances to leave home. Frances, mother was so much of a hoarder that her father had to sleep in hotels. Her father had affairs. Her father slept with call girls and anything else that breathe. Men or woman, it didn't matter.

Weeping, Frances jumped up when she heard Carlos call her name.

"What the hell are you doing here?" Frances asked in an unfriendly tone.

Carlos shuffled his feet." I came to help."

"Help! Damn you have some nerve! You are the one that turned me in. If you wanted to help me, you would have done so a long time ago." Frances laughed until her sides hurt.

Carlos was dumfound at the words and mad laughter that spilled out of Frances' mouth. For it was the same mad laughter, Carlos had heard coming from his mentally ill mother.

"If I give to someone who is poor in wealth, spirit, health or faith without Love in my heart, then who is really the poor man?" Frances finally said.

"Frances, what do you mean?" Carlos asked.

"You don't have love for anyone but your damn self and that slut Alice!" Frances started laughing again.

When Frances laughter died down, Carlos once again tried to talk with her in a gentle matter. "Frances, when we have peace in our hearts and minds, we draw peace into our lives. When discord and disharmony present themselves, we can stand firm. When we let go of the need to prove ourselves, nothing and no one can disturb the quiet and peace of our minds. I don't have much money in my bank account, but I will use it to bail you out. I really want to help you. You are my friend. You have always been kind to Alice and me."

Carlos spoke the truth. Frances had always been so kind to him and Alice. As a matter of fact, Frances was the one that brought the couple together.

It was a summer day. The small town Collage had been hosting an open house.

Alice and Frances had meet the weekend before at a local diner. They hit it. Over apple pie and coffee, they chatted away like old friends. More like sisters.

At the College, the following weekend Carlos had caught Alice's eye as he stood behind an Oak tree smoking.

Alice had always been drawn to that type of bad boy. Alice had a hidden wild side.

"Alice, you like him don't you?" Frances snapped Alice out of her day dream. "How can I not? He is hot!" Alice smiled.

Frances didn't need to hear another word, she took Alice by the arm and introduced the pair.

Carlos, had his share of girlfriends before but had never met anyone as wonderful, kind and beautiful as Alice. From the first smile Alice flashed at Carlos all other woman ceased to exist in Carlos world.

For Carlos, Alice turned darkness into light. She changed Carlos life with her first hello. Carlos allowed Alice to see the real him. He opened his gentle heart and made room for her. She healed his wounds with her love.

Within you shines a light radiant, pure. A light untouched by circumstances, unscathed by fear, unaffected by judgment; immutable, immortal, perfect light. So strong is this essence, so pure is this presence that even in the blackest moments, you illuminate the darkness, you shine through the night, beaming with pure love, you make this world bright. Clearly I see it, and truly I know: you are the light of Love. Alice taught Carlos that love lesson.

Carlos taught her this one-Your life's story may tell of pain and sadness, loss and grief, separation and lack, regret and wrongdoing. Hear not this story! Listen now instead: You are the essence of grace, you are the spirit of hope. You are the called and the chosen, you are innocent, pure. You are whole, and healed, abundant, and free. Simply, eternally, completely, YOU are Love. Shine on!

Carlos and Alice feel in love quickly. Alice accepted his proposal only a month after their first date.

It was Frances who helped Carlos buy the pear-shaped engagement ring at a Mom and Pop jewelry store.

It was Frances who helped Carlos plan the romantic proposal. A proposal that indeed would make any woman's heart melt. A picnic out in the country that included red roses, fried chicken and a hot air balloon ride. A proposal all funded by Frances.

Frances, Carlos and Alice became the best of friends but neither Carlos or Frances knew about the wounds the other had on their hearts.

On a windy July 4th night, as the sounds of booming fireworks echoed in the air Carlos dressed in blue, Alice dressed in white and Frances dressed in red headed to City Hall.

In front of an overweight, sweaty and balding judge Carlos and Alice wed.

Declaring their Undying love to each other, Carlos and Alice sweetly kissed after exchanging simple sliver bands.

Carlos showed his softer side and recited a poem as part of his wedding vows. He said," I pray you will take a deep breath of joy, and fill your heart with ease. I pray you will see angels, signs, wonders and miracles. I pray on this day, and always,

 You will know peace. Please know that I am thankful for you. YOU bless this world with your light, your smile, your presence. I love you Alice."

In return Alice said,"

To reach heaven within we must experience hell within... To become enlightened one has to be free from their own darkness and one cannot be free from darkness without making the darkness conscious.

We all have a choice to make this life into a Heaven on earth or a Hell on earth and once we have experienced Hell a few times, I can assure you Heaven is a much better option and it can be achieved here and now in this lifetime... if we believe it's possible. I do. I love you Carlos forever."

"Get out of here! Judaist! How could you betray me like you did!" Frances started to pull out her own hair.

"Frances, don't do that you are going to hurt yourself. Please sit down. Let's talk. There is something you don't know about me. Something I should have told you a long time ago. My mom, she is sick like you Frances. I try to act tough, all macho, like nothing in this world can pierce my soul, like I don't need anyone, but that's all an act. I do what I do for her. To support her. I see your pain. I know, I lived it. Let me help you Frances please. I care!" Carlos' brown eyes shined with compassion and warmth.

Frances stopped pacing then. "Your mom is sick like me? Does she hear voices telling her to do bad things too?"

"Sometimes." Carlos answered honestly. His eyes then shifted downward. Carlos mumbled," Sometimes the voices even told her to hurt me."

Frances started to grind her teeth then." Hurt you? Why would a mother do that?"

"Sometimes Frances my mom did hurt me, but with help my mom got better. She now lives in a nursing home , has friends and lives a full and active life.

Frances you can get help. You can live a blessed life also." Carlos replied.

"My dad doesn't even have a bed to sleep in." Frances blurred out in all the confusion.

"What do you mean?" Carlos asked concerned.

The big guard that had been watching Frances and Carlos said," Time is up! You will have to visit your crazy friend another day."

Carlos promised Frances he would help her in any way he could before he left.

By mid-afternoon the Collage campus was buzzing with all the news headlines. Frances deep seeded secrets had spilled out. On the front page of the local paper was a picture of Frances' childhood home full of rats, bugs and trash. The local dump looked cleaner and more organized.

Alice flopped into her bath tub that was filled with her favorite brand of rose scented bubble bath.

Alice felt all the tension building in her head. As if she didn't feel bad enough about what happened with Jimmy, now she had to read about the horrors her best friend endured. Could this day get any worse?

Alice sunk down lower in the soapy water. "God, I know I haven't talked to you in a very long time. I know it must sound funny hearing my voice, but I need you. I am so confused about everything. I love Carlos so much but seeing Jimmy again has brought up feelings that I long had forgotten. How could I be so caught up in my world, that I couldn't see Frances' world crumbling? Please help me sort this all out."

Carlos knew as he left the jail, he would have to move his drug supply and fast if he were to help Frances and his mother. He also knew he would not be able to come home to Alice that night. Carlos thought about something Alice once said to him.

They were walking alone in the woods looking at the changing fall leaves shortly after they got married. Alice turned to Carlos saying," Our words, and our thoughts are like seeds. From the moment in which we bring them out, and sow them into the ground around us. At first the seeds may be quiet, as if they were dead, as if they have no life of their own. But they have. To the extent that we keep feeding them, they grow, they become increasingly strong as they take roots and reach out to touch the lives of others. Are you planting strong healthy thoughts to be shared with all others?"

Alice's words haunted Carlos. He wanted to live a clean, crime-free life. But selling drugs was all he ever knew. He started selling drugs as a way to fed and clothe himself when he was just a mere kid. Then he had to sell them to pay for the nursing home his mother was in. Then when he married Alice, to give her the things she desired.

Carlos tried to go straight once. But no one would hire him for a 9 to 5 job with his record. Carlos had no other choice he felt. But he was wrong. God had big plans for him.

Jimmy felt something stir in his spirit, something prompted him to pick up his notes and re-read the story he was sharing with his English Lit class. As he was reading his own notes, something struck him, his story could help his classmates every one of them.

Jimmy felt a fire burn within him. A new, unexpected and thrilling feeling. Jimmy's life purpose became clear in that moment. He was to become a counselor.

Jimmy pulled out of his wallet, his father's picture. Kissing it, Jimmy said," Thank you

Dad." He then marched off to Bruce's office feeling happy.

"Sunshine- Chapter Three"

Carlos knew Alice would be furious when he snuck into his dorm room window at 3am.

Alice stood in a   pink night gown and bathrobe with her hands on her hips. "Where have you been? I have been worried sick!" Alice was breathing fire. Her nostrils flared like a roaring lion. Her bottom lip quivered like she was about to cry. Alice's eyes burned with a wildfire of righteous anger.

Carlos ran a hand over his face." Please baby, I have had a long day. Can we talk about this later?"

"Like Hell we will! You were out selling dope again! Weren't you?" Alice poked a finger into Carlos' chest.

"Baby, Please calm down. There is a reason behind all this madness. I had to move the product because I needed to raise some bail money for Frances and pay for my Mom's room again this month. I am so sorry Honey, I wish there was another way." Carlos dropped to his knees to beg for forgiveness.

Alice dropped down on her knees also. Embracing Carlos she said," There has got to be a better way. We can't go on like this."

"I know. There has got to be a better way. But I can't pay the bills since my grandfather cut me off. Grandfather threated to put me in jail if I don't finish collage . And he already hates my mom." Carlos now weeping said.

"Then we should use plan B. I will drop out of school and get a job." Alice kissing her husband's tears said.

Carlos waved his hands wildly." No! I will not hear of it! You have to much talent to drop out of school. We will figure this out." Carlos said in his most believable voice.

Alice did have talent. When she was a young girl she used to entertain her mother and Jimmy with her wonderful stories weaved of faith, friendship and happy endings.

One day Alice was watching TV. Alice's eyes lit up when she saw Katie Couric on the news. Alice found her dream of becoming a reporter in that moment.

In spite of her horrible upbringing Alice was a success in H.S. Alice got five scholarships when she graduated, but it did not pay for all her Collage costs.

Alice looked Carlos in the eyes." I don't know how you do it." She said.

"Do what baby?" Carlos asked. "Those eyes of yours could sell me the Brooklyn Bridge. How could I ever stay mad at you?" Alice said.

Carlos' face lit up with a bright smile then. "And you my dear have much too much sunshine in your soul to walk in anyone's shadow. That's why I am not letting you quit school."

"So I guess we are back to square one again. What are we going to do Honey seriously?" Alice asked concerned.

"Frist, we are going to bail Frances out. Second we are going to find her a good lawyer and doctor. She really needs help." Carlos sadly said.

"Carlos, have you seen the papers? Her childhood home was a house of horrors. I mean we had it bad but nothing like Frances went through. They are finding dead dogs all over the house." Alice began to weep.

Once again Carlos pulled Alice close." It's going to be o.k. We will help Frances."

What the young couple didn't know was that help was all-ready on the way to Frances.

Four-foot-nine, spunky, tan , blond and blue eyed Sara Wilson, super mom, lawyer, advocate, and proud church member packed a suitcase filled with dress attire , law books and hair spray boarded a plane .

When Jimmy called her directly at midnight, Sara knew she had to help.

Sara was very close to Jimmy. She was Jimmy's mom.

Sara got off her plane at 5:45 am. She was tried , hungry and cold but she still looked like a polished jewel. Sara was a graceful and beautiful woman.

Sara grabbed her suitcase. Then walked through the double doors of the small airport.

Sara hailed a cab. The cabbie stopped in front of the curb for her, slamming on his brakes. The cabbie was not even on duty but he could not deny this beautiful woman a ride. For her presence demanded attention.

"Where to Miss?" The cabbie asked in a friendly Scottish accent.

Sara replied, "To the Collage Campus please."

The cabbie knew the campus well. He had two daughters that attended the Collage. "Yes, Miss." The cabbie replied. Trying to make small talk the cabbie asked," Are you a reporter doing a story about the nut case that planned to blow up the school?"

Sara frowned at the man's comment. The man said," I am sorry if I offended you. It's just that my two daughters go to that College and well it would have killed me if anything happened to them."

Sara smiled saying," I understand but everyone needs a little bit of compassion. Sometimes people can't see what is going on behind closed doors to make someone feel so much pain that they would want to hurt innocent people."

"Yes, you are right but how do we protect our children from violence if we don't even know who is lurking at our backdoors?" The cabbie asked.

"I think what everyone needs to learn is how to love. Once we learn how to give it unconditionally, wounds will start to heal and the world will be a much kinder place to live in. If everyone watched out for their fellow man like they watched out for themselves this world would be a much better place." Sara stated.

The cabbie dropped Sara off near the entrance of Jimmy's dorm. Sara gave the cabbie a big tip before exiting the cab.

As Sara knocked on Jimmy's door, Jimmy who was studying hard jumped at the loud knock. He was not expecting anyone to come this early.

Jimmy, opened the door." Mom! Is that really you! I didn't think I would see you again so soon."

Jimmy hugged Sara with a bear hug. "Don't worry Jumbo, Mama's on the case. I just wanted to come by and say a quick "Hello." I don't want to cramp your style. I am going to go to the jail now and see what's up with your classmate. Are you free for lunch?" Sara asked.

Jimmy said, "Of course I am free. "But then Jimmy recalled his study date with Alice. "Oh Darn! I promised Alice I would help her study."

"Wait! Alice, Alice? Your self-proclaimed soulmate? She's attending Collage here?" Sara asked shocked.

"She's not my Alice, Mom. But yes, it's the Alice I knew a lifetime ago."

Sara wagged her eyebrows. "Oh I see. So she is your Alice."

"It's not like that at all mom. I am just helping her study. Really." Jimmy replied.

"Of course you are son. Your father and I used to "study" a lot too." Sara said smiling.

Jimmy rolled his eyes." Whatever."

"How about dinner then?" Sara asked.

"It's a date." Jimmy replied.

Sara hugged Jimmy again." I will call you later." She said before leaving Jimmy's room.

Leon met up with Carlos behind a large Oak tree.

"Leon, I am counting on you to get the rest of the supply sold by the afternoon. If you don't get arrested like you did last time, there will be a bonus in it for you." Carlos said.

Leon's face lit up then." You got it Boss man." Leon replied.

Carlos and Leon split up quickly when they saw Bruce walking through the parking lot.

Bruce was tried. He had been up all night praying for all the students. He was worried about how Frances arrest would affect them all. His spirit was anxious. He knew his students would have a difficult time getting over this.

Bruce walked to his office with his head hung low. He nearly walked into a tree because he was so distracted.

When he reached his office, he was surprised to see Jimmy waiting for him. "Good Morning Jimmy." Bruce said with a forced smile.

"Not such a good morning. I didn't sleep a wink last night." Jimmy replied.

"I thought you were feeling better after we talked. I know it's a tough time for everyone, but keep this in mind, Today, I choose not to take my life for granted. I choose not to look upon the fact that I am healthy, have food in my refrigerator and have clean water to drink as givens. They are not givens for so many people in our world. The fact that I am safe and (relatively) sane are not givens. That I was born into a family who loves me and into a country not ravaged by war are not givens. It is impossible to name all of the circumstances in my life I've taken for granted. All of the basic needs I've had met, all of the friendships and job opportunities and financial blessings and the list, truly, is endless. The fact that I am breathing is a miracle, one I too rarely stop to appreciate.

I'm stopping, right now, to be grateful for everything I am and everything I've been given. I'm stopping, right now, to be grateful for every pleasure and every pain that has contributed to the me who sits here and writes these words.

I am thankful for my life. This moment is a blessing. Each breathe a gift. That I've been able to take so much for granted is a gift, too. But it's not how I want to live -not when gratitude is an option, not when wonder and awe are choices. I choose gratitude. I choose wonder. I choose awe. I choose everything that suggests I'm opening myself to the miraculous reality of simply being alive for one moment more." Bruce said.

"I feel great about finally choosing a career path, but there is something you don't know about Alice." Jimmy replied.

"Well Jimmy, Woman can be complex. Do you want to talk about it?" Bruce asked.

"I really would like too but the pain is just too fresh." Jimmy replied.

"Well, Jimmy if you ever need to talk I am here for you day or night!" Bruce said.

"Thanks, if you don't mind I just like to hang out here for a while. Oh by the way, my mom is here. I called her last night. I figured she may be able to help Frances."

"That's a good idea Jimmy. I would have hired a lawyer for her but a professor's salary only goes so far." Bruce said.

After posting Frances $200,000 bail, Sara met with her new client.

Sara saw the signs of mental illness in Frances.

Frances was full of anger, could not answer simple questions and could not focus.

"Frances, we are going to get you help. I promise you." Sara said as her heart filled with compassion for the lost woman.

"Can, I go home now?' Frances asked.

Sara felt a lump form in her chest. It felt like her heart was breaking.

Frances parents had disowned her.

Trying to explain to Frances gently that she no longer had a home to go back too, Frances collapsed into a puddle of tears.

"It's going to be all right sweetie. I am going to help you." Sara patted Frances on her back.

"I do bad things. Mother said," Every time you put something positive into the universe, the world changes. Your kindness invites miracles to show up, not just in your world, but in the whole world. But when your soul is dark everyone hates you. Mother used to lock me in the closet with rats when I told her about the voices in my head." Frances tearfully shared.

"I promise you no one will ever do that to you again." Sara promised.

Jimmy once again stood in front of his classmates. His heart felt heavy as he saw Frances' empty chair.

"I left off by telling you my dad had met a boy name Frenchie. And that Frenchie changed my dad's life. You see my dad met Frenchie during the Civil Rights Movement. As little as my father was, he knew Frenchie was not being treated right.

One day Frenchie and my dad was out in front of the ghetto shelter playing with an old baseball they had found. My grandma and Frenchie's mama were sitting on the front steps watching the boys play, when a group of very mean, very scary white men started harassing

Frenchie and his mother. They kicked Frenchie but what they did to Frenchie's mother was so much worse. They started trying to rape her. My grandma begged them to stop. But what could a blind woman do to stop those men? Frenchie started crying.

But courage bubbled up in my six year old's father's heart! "Stop it!" He yelled. "Stop hurting my aunt!"

The men laughed at my dad. They ripped Frenchie's mother's dress.

"I told you to stop it!" My father yelled at the top of his lungs. My father stumped on one of the man's foot. "Leave my Aunt alone!" My father yelled again. He then started throwing rocks at the men.

Frenchie by this time gathered his courage and began throwing rocks also.

The one man slapped my father crossed the face, but my dad didn't cry.

"I told you to leave my Aunt alone! You mean Mister! "My father screamed again. He then took a broom stick and started swinging it wildly chasing the men away.

Because Frenchie was black, my dad had a terrible time growing up. He was beaten many times over. My dad, grandma, uncle and Frenchie and his mom ended up homeless again because my dad would not dissolve his friendship with Frenchie."

"With no money, no support, no one but each other, the five of them lived in the woods. They moved from place to place. They stole food and clothing but only when they had too. This went on for years. Eventually, you will come to understand that Love heals everything, and Love is all there is. The journey may take many lifetimes, but you will complete it. It is impossible not to complete it. It is not a question of if but of when. Every situation you create serves this purpose. Every experience you encounter serves this purpose."

Leon gasped at that." You mean your dad respected and loved a black man so much during the Civil Rights Movement, that he actually risked his own life to protect his friend? I don't think I have ever had anyone love me that much. What ended up happening to all of them?" Leon asked.

"After two years of living in the woods, steeling and fighting for their lives, they met a Baptist preacher that took them in and loved them like his own. But tragic events struck once again. Frenchie's mom died of the flu. And Frenchie himself was ripped away by an angry mob." Jimmy got a far off look in his eye then.

Leon got up and excused himself from the class room.

"Excuse me everyone. I need to go talk to Leon." Jimmy said walking out of the classroom next.

Leon got into Collage on a grant. Leon did not have an easy life. He too wanted to better himself.

Leon's mother was a drug addict that overdosed when Leon was only a year old.

Leon's father was not much better. He was out of work the most of the time. He was a man with a bad temper.

When Leon was only six years old, Leon was ripped away from his dad by a social worker on Christmas day because his father was arrested from beating his girlfriend.

Leon rose against the odds. While in foster care he became an A student, a talented baseball player and an honor student.

He graduated H.S. with honors. Leon was a good kid in spite of his harsh upbringing. He never did drugs, or drank. That was until he met Carlos.

Leon met Carlos right after he had graduated H.S. Leon had turned 18. He was no longer allowed to live in the foster home.

Leon was late on his rent. Carlos made Leon an offer he could not refuse. Selling drugs went against ever fiber in Leon's being, but he saw no other way out.

From the moment Leon made his first sale, he got addicted to the fast money.

At times, Leon's behavior was even more thuggish then Carlos.

"Leon, are you all right?" Jimmy asked in a quiet voice.

"Why, do you care? We are not friends!" Leon trying to hide his tears said.

"Leon, I do care. I affirm for you that the Spirit of Love and the Presence of Hope opens wide your heart to your Divinity and to the sacred light in all those around you. I affirm a profound level of wholeness, wellness, and oneness that transcends physicality and centers you in the heart of God. I affirm for you angels, abundance, and acceptance. I affirm for you that all is well. I affirm for you Love, peace and happiness. I may not be much but I am a friend." Jimmy replied.

Leon slowly turned around to face Jimmy. Leon's eyes were beat red.

Jimmy knew Leon had been crying hard.

"Thank you. I know I and Carlos have been downright brutal to you. We both owe you an apology. It's really nice to know someone cares. You are all-right in my book." Leon said smiling.

Jimmy felt heat rush to his cheeks. "Are you feeling better?" Jimmy asked once again in a shy voice.

"Yeah. Yeah I am." Leon answered before walking back into class. Jimmy followed.

Everyone's attention shifted to them.

Carlos mouthed to Leon," What the hell happened?"

Leon mouthed back," I'll tell you later."

Jimmy returned to the head of the class." I apologize for the short delay. My dad was heartbroken after Frenchie vanished. He became troublesome and very hard for my grandma to handle."

"The good preacher saw my dad needed a father so he wed my grandma. He didn't love her but my grandma needed him, my dad and uncle needed him. It was at that time, my father was introduced to God and structure, rules and a belt. My father hated it."

"Why? At least he had parents that gave a damn about him!" Carlos chimed in.

"Well Carlos, think about it. He never really had a "dad", he had just lost his best friend. He was scared." Jimmy shared.

"What did he do?" Carlos asked.

"Well let's see. To be totally honest when my dad turned 13, he got involved in drugs. I mean hard-core drugs. My dad ran away from home." Jimmy supplied.

"Are you serious? "Alice asked wide-eyed and shocked.

"Dead serious. My dad totally rebelled. He rebelled against my grandma, his step-dad, his brother and the world. But most of all against God." Jimmy shared.

Bruce standing in the back of the class could see the students were becoming emotional engaged in Jimmy's story. He could also see that Jimmy was breaking out of his shell. Jimmy had captured his classmate's hearts.

Bruce silently thanked God for the miracles he was seeing.

"I can't understand why your dad would turn against God." Carlos said shocking everyone. Seeing the shock on everyone's faces, Carlos added," That's right! I do believe in God!"

The revelation left everyone speechless.

"Every time you put something positive into the universe, the world changes. Your kindness invites miracles to show up, not just in your world, but in the whole world. My dad didn't understand that until later in his life. My dad was 15 when he returned home, but he was not the same person. He was hard, he lost his boyish nature. He had changed his look. He was now covered in tattoos. My grandma tried to accept my dad. She forgive him. My uncle and my grandma's husband however felt the deep hurt of my father's abandonment. The tension in the household became unbearable. My uncle who always shadowed my dad, tried making up for lost time. He loved his brother. But dad resented a little kid crowding his space. This caused even more anger and heartache. My grandma started getting sick from all the stress."

"My grandma's husband felt buried under the pressure and stress. But had an idea. He would take my grandma on the honey moon she never had.

Knowing that my grandma would never leave her boys without having them under the care of a loving adult, the preacher hired an older lady from his church to "Babysit." The boys.

The woman had a daughter named Sara. She was a pretty little girl. Sara was bright and bubbly. She was angelic like and a year younger then my dad.

The first time my dad met her, he was smitten. He anticipated what it would be to kiss her soft lips that shimmered with pink lipstick. What it would be like to put a smile on her pretty face. What it would be like to dance with her.

But young Sara knew about my dad's background. She wanted nothing to do with my dad. My dad worked hard to mend his wild ways. My dad began going to church and reading the bible. He thought that would impress Sara. However Sara saw through my dad's plan.

My dad then got a job helping a local farmer. He fed the chickens and cleaned the stables. Dad thought that having a little money in his pocket would win over Sara but it didn't.

Sara's brush offs only made my dad want her more.

Dad found out that Sara loved flowers. So when my grandma and the preacher wanted to plant a garden, dad jumped at the chance to help them.

The preacher was so happy. So was my grandma.

"It was the middle of spring. Dad was working in the garden. A ladybug landed on my dad's hand. Dad looked down at it. Suddenly his eyes filled with tears as he felt the very real, very tangible presence of God. God's love filled my dad's soul in that moment. He felt God embracing him in that moment."

Jimmy's classmates and Bruce sat perfectly still. They hung on Jimmy's every word.

"Dad began to live again in that moment. He was freed from the burden of his sadness, the moment he gave it to God. When Dad found himself again, Sara saw the beauty inside his soul. Sara saw the man that dad had always been, the man God created him to be. Sara and Dad began dating."

Alice glanced loving over at Carlos in that moment. Alice saw the man that the world could not see. She saw Carlos' loving heart.

The way Alice looked at Carlos made Jimmy's stomach turn. Jimmy was so in love with her.

Alice then said," Everyone is connect by the need to be loved. How did your dad propose to your mom?"

Jimmy smiled." Well a lot happened between their first date and their wedding day, and I'll share that with you tomorrow."

As Jimmy was walking out of the classroom, he caught the happiness that shined in Bruce's eyes.

"Baby, Is Jimmy helping you study today?" Carlos asked Alice as they walked out of the classroom hand and hand.

"Yes." Alice answered, as she took notice that Carlos didn't call Jimmy anything else but his given name.

"O.K. sweetness. I will be home early tonight. I am going to stop by to see my mom. Then I have some errands to run." Carlos replied.

Alice's eye brows shot up. "Errands? What kind of errands?"

"It's not the kind that will get me into any trouble. I am going to look for a job." Carlos replied.

Alice's started jumping up and down." Really? That's great. I'm so happy!"

"Yes, sweetie. Please stop jumping up and down. Play it cool. You are drawing attention to us." Carlos blushing said.

Alice stopped. A wide smile spread a crossed her face. "Do you know long I prayed for this? Carlos , you have just become the man God always wanted you to be."

"Honey, it's because of you that I became any kind of man at all. From the moment I met you, I wanted to become a better person. I saw your light and I wanted to be part of that." Carlos admitted.

Alice's love for Carlos became cemented in her heart at that moment. There in the middle of the campus, Alice announced to everyone within ear shot that Carlos was her husband.

"Shush Baby. I know you are excited but can we talk about this later sweetie. I don't want you to lose your scholarship you got. And you know what will happen if they find out your married to a drug dealer." Carlos said concerned.

"Former. You are no longer that man." Alice laughed. She kissed Carlos saying," I'll see you later."

"O.K. Baby." Carlos replied as he walked off.

Sara got Frances settled into a cheap hotel room. Sara didn't know if Frances could handle what she would soon be facing. A firestorm of reporters, an angry local mob and of course a trial.

Sara was worried about her new client.

Frances was so confused. She looked up at Sara with her big doe eyes. She asked," Am I going to live here forever? Because if I am I will have to put tin foil on the window- They read your thoughts you know? You can't trust the government. They have spies all over. They put little tiny camera's inside your head so they can read your inter-most-thoughts. The only way to stop them is with tin foil. It blocks the camera's signal."

Sara sat down next to Frances. Sara gently patted her hand. "We talked about this on the car ride here. You have to stay here until we figure this all out. We will have to talk to a judge. Do you recall me telling you that?"

"No! I don't. I am sorry. I don't remember. See they are tapping into my mind. They are trying to make me confused. They are plotting against me. I can hear them now. Are you my friend?" Frances replied.

"Yes, I am your friend. I have to go out for a little while, but I promise to come back as soon as I can." Sara replied.

"Where are you going?" Frances asked like a scared child talking to her mommy.

"I am going to go get you something to eat, a tooth brush and some clothing. I am going to give you my cell phone number so you can call me if you get scared ok." Sara softly smiled.

Frances replied," O.K."

Sara took out a slip of paper and a pen from her purse. She jotted down the number. She then handed it to Frances.

"Remember Frances, you have to stay here. This is where I will come back too so if you leave this room, I won't know how to find you. I am going to turn the T.V. on so you can watch it when I am gone." Sara said.

Sara turned on the T.V., Frances eyes got wide and she began to laugh as she saw that an I love Lucy Marathon was on.

"I like this show. That lady is funny." Frances said like a child.

"Maybe I will bring back some chips and soda and we can stay up all night watching it." Sara smiled.

"Really? My Mommy never let me watch T.V." Frances admitted.

"Yes, of course, we are friends! That's what girlfriends do. We can have a sleep over." Sara said heading towards the door.

"Hi, Jimmy." Alice said in a light and cheery tone.

Jimmy, who was sitting on a bench with his nose buried in a book looked up. "Oh, Hey." Jimmy response was cold.

"I want to thank you again for helping me. I also want to say sorry about before. I didn't want you to find out that I was married to Carlos in that matter." Alice said.

"Your life. Your business. Why don't we just get to studying? I really don't have

anything else to talk to you about."
Jimmy said wounded.

"O.K. if that's the way you want it." Alice
replied.

The two of them walked in silence to the
other side of campus. They reached the
library.

Jimmy, still a gentleman held a glass door
open for Alice.

Alice's high heels clicked on the blue tile
floor of the library.

The librarian, a grouchy older woman with
white hair and a wrinkled face that
looked like a prune looked up with a
warning as the pair passed her desk.

Jimmy and Alice tried to walk more quietly towards a group of tables located in the back of the library.

Jimmy, always clumsy walked into a young woman carrying a stack of books, making them spill all over the floor.

Alice and Jimmy bent down at the same time to help the woman pick up the books and ended banging his head.

Alice let out an "Ouch."

The librarian now stood over them saying," If you can't be quiet, go study somewhere else!"

She then walked back to her desk. As soon as she returned to her desk, Alice stuck out her tongue and made a funny face to mock the woman.

Jimmy's mind flooded with memories of the younger version of Alice. The Alice who was his best friend. The Alice he was in love with.

Jimmy recalled Alice's fifth birthday. Jimmy and his parents arrived early to Alice's home.

Sara wanted to help Alice's mother set up for the party. Because they were best friends, there was no need for Sara to knock on the front door. She just walked right in.

When the trio walked in, they saw Alice and her mom having a power struggle. Alice had wanted to wear mismatched shoes, a princess toy crown and a Summer dress in the middle of winter.

Alice's mom however had another plan.

Alice stumped her feet all the way back to her bedroom when her mother made her change.

Alice stuck out her tongue every time her mother turned her back.

Alice had always been head-strong, spirited and as stubborn as a mule.

Actually those where the qualities Jimmy loved about Alice.

Jimmy was very embarrassed by the whole incident that took place in the Library.

However Alice didn't leave. She found a table to sit at. Jimmy meekly followed Alice to the table.

Jimmy and Alice studied together for hours. Neither of they knew, they were renewing a lifelong friendship that had been robbed from them.

Carlos frustration built a fire inside his soul like glowing ambers.

Carlos had gone on ten job interviews that afternoon. He had been laughed at, thrown out of one office and refused a job application at another.

Carlos was about to give up, when he remembered Alice's sweet smile and how excited she was.

Carlos was walking down the Street with his hands in his jean pockets, when he noticed a Help Wanted Sign in a gas station.

Carlos saw a man seated on an old dirty plastic lawn chair dressed in blue overalls. The man was drinking a cold soda. The man's hands were full of grease. The man in his 60's had kind- gentle- grey eyes, a soft smile and salt and pepper colored hair.

"Excuse me sir." Carlos said getting the man's attention.

"May I help you?" The man who had the name Buck on his overalls asked.

"Yes, I was wondering if you are still hiring." Carlos asked.

"Can you push a broom?" Buck asked.

"Sure." Carlos replied.

"I can only pay five bucks an hour. If you can fit in the overalls, hanging on the hook in my office , you got the job. Be here at six am." Buck replied.

Carlos shook the man's hand in a firm grip. "Thank you, Mr. Buck. By the way my name is Carlos."

Buck replied," I know who you are."

Normally those words would have sent Carlos into attack mode, but there was something about the way Buck said it. His tone didn't sound like an accusation, it just sounded like a simple statement.

Carlos started to walk away, when Buck called him back. "Hey kid you forgot the overalls."

"Oh, Yeah right." Carlos said blushing.

Carlos followed Buck into the office.

The small and cozy gas station office was very clean.

Inside the office was a small desk that had an organized stack of work orders, a stapler, paper clips, pens and a phone on it.

Behind the desk was a chair. There was also a picture of a younger-looking Buck in an Army uniform and another man hanging in a gold frame on the wall.

A few plastic chairs stood like solders on the other side of the room. There was also a coat rack with overalls hanging on it.

But what surprised Carlos the most was the pocket-sized bible sticking out of the back pocket of Buck's overalls.

Buck handed Carlos the overalls. Then he took Carlos breath away." This book was written by my favorite author, why don't you read it then give it a review." Buck handed Carlos his bible.

Carlos believed in God, but never read the bible before.

When Carlos was a little boy, his mother had a beautiful bible. The front cover of the bible depicted a scene of angels. His mother's name was engraved in gold of the front cover.

 Carlos loved that bible.

One day Carlos went into the dresser drawer where that bible laid. Carlos mother warned him never to touch it.

Carlos, age seven lifted the cover of the bible with his fat little fingers. He didn't know his mother was standing behind him.

Without warning, his mother ripped the bible out of his hands. She tore out ever last page.

Carlos and his mother were living with Carlos' brutally cruel grandfather at that time. Hearing what was happening, Carlos' grandfather marched into the room.

Carlos' mother was screaming like a mad woman.

It was at that moment that Carlos' grandfather admitted that his daughter was ill. Something he had been denying all along.

It was that very night Carlos' mother was abandon at the State Mental Center.

Carlos was pulled back into the present moment by Buck's voice. "Go on son, take it."

Carlos was dumfounded." I can't." Carlos cried.

"Sure you can. Go on now son, Take it." Buck once again instructed.

Carlos reached for the bible like it was a bomb. "I'll see you in the morning." Buck said as Carlos left the office.

Buck watched troubled Carlos from his office window.

Carlos stopped on the sidewalk in front of the gas station. He looked at the bible that felt like a foreign object in his hands. "I don't know why you lead me here God, but I am going to try to trust you."

Carlos said as he started walking again it started to rain lightly.

The cool rain felt refreshing and healing on Carlos' skin. At that moment, Carlos felt in his spirit the presence of God engulf him in love , peace and joy.

Carlos knew at that moment somehow everything would work out.

When Carlos reached the bus stop, instead of taking the bus to go back to campus, he took the bus to see his very ill mother.

Raina stared out the window at the pouring rain. Dressed in a flimsy night gown and thin robe, Raina tried to count the raindrops.

Raina was once a very beautiful woman. She now looked twice her age. Her tan skin was covered with wrinkles. Her brown hair had a big bald spot from where she had pulled it out. Her make-up was smeared all over her face. Her bones were visible from not eating.

Raina grew angry as she lost count of the rain drops.

Carlos desperately tried to gain his mother's attention by clapping his hands.

"Mom, did you hear what I said? You have to eat your lunch otherwise the doctors will be forced to insert a feeding tube again. I already gave him permission to Mother." Carlos struggled to explain.

Raina just laughed.

"Mom, will you please take a few bites of this yummy salad." Carlos begged.

Raina took a bite of the salad, but didn't sallow it. Instead she spit it in her son's face.

Carlos didn't yell or scream. He picked up the napkin and wiped his face.

"Mom, would you like to try some of this applesauce?" Carlos asked.

Raina's face lit up like fireworks." Apple sauce good!" She said.

Carlos dipped a clean spoon into the applesauce. He fed his mother like a baby.

The only thing she ate was the applesauce. But when there was none left, Raina got angry. She started swinging at Carlos.

Carlos caught his mother's arms. "Mom, I love you. I am going home now. But Alice and I will be by to visit again soon."

"Carlos? I love you my son." Raina replied. She then said," We all have the ability with us to turn our lives from a hell into a heaven, when we believe in ourselves as Spirit. Infuse your life with action. Don't wait for it to happen. Make it happen. Make your own future. Create from your own hope and inspiration. Be love. And whatever your beliefs, honor yourself, not by passively waiting for grace to come down from upon high, but by doing what you can to make grace happen yourself. Right now, right down here on Earth."

Suddenly the light of recognition faded from Raina's eyes. She began chasing Carlos around the room." Get out of here! You are trying to poison me!" Raina screamed.

Carlos made it out of the room safely. As he passed the nurse's station, the charge nurse asked," Did you get Raina to eat anything?"

"Just applesauce. Do what you have to do to keep my mother from starving please. "Carlos begged.

The nurse needed no further explanation from Carlos. She knew it was time to hook Raina to a feeding tube as they had done many times before.

"I'm sorry Carlos." The nurse replied.

Carlos said nothing as he walked back out into the pouring rain. This time the rain felt like small but powerful needles prinking his skin. It was cold and uncomfortable. Just like the time he had been spending with his mother was becoming harder, colder and more painful.

"Wow, it's nearly dinner time! I've got to get going. I am meeting my mom for dinner. She is helping Frances." Jimmy reviled.

"Really? That's awesome news! Carlos will be happy- He was going to- Never mind. Your mom is an angel!" Alice said in a joyful tone.

"Mom, is doing what comes naturally to her. She has a gift of helping others." Jimmy's face beamed with a radiant glow.

"We better get going then. Will you be free to help me study again tomorrow?" Alice asked.

"Sure. What time?" Jimmy replied.

"Is after dinner time ok?" Alice asked.

"Sure, let's make it for seven." Jimmy said as he scooped up his study notes into a neat pile and put them in his book bag.

"It's a date." Alice replied.

The two of them walked out of the library together. They then went their separate ways as they reached the front lawn.

Jimmy was walking back to his dorm room when his cell phone rang. He saw on the caller I.D. that it was his mother calling. Jimmy answered the phone.

"Hi, Honey, I am really sorry to do this to you but can we take a rain check on dinner. Frances really needs me. I am swamped preparing her case." Sara downtrodden asked.

"How is Frances holding up mom? We are all really concerned." Jimmy replied.

Sara sighed," Bad son. She is very confused. Very ill. She has a long difficult journey ahead. Her parents want nothing to do with her. They won't even return my calls."

"Mom, is there anything I can do to help? "Jimmy always a soft-heart asked.

"Hope- Chapter Five"

"Pray for Frances Sweetie. Frances is in serious trouble. God has to help us." Sara sighed.

"I will Mom. I will pray. I am also going to take to Facebook and Twitter to start a prayer chain for her." Jimmy shared.

"Jimmy, you're a good man, just like your daddy. I am so proud of you son." Sara replied.

"I am nothing like dad. Dad was brave, strong and courageous. He was a real hero. I am weak, clumsy, and a nerd." Jimmy sadly said.

"Jimmy! You are just like your dad. You are funny, sweet, loving and smart. Someday a woman will be lucky to have you as her husband."

"Oh Mom. Thanks. You always know how to make me feel better." Jimmy replied.

"Listen sweetie, I am almost at the hotel, can I give you a   call later?" Sara asked.

"Yes, by all means." Jimmy replied. "I love you."

"Love you too soon. Kisses." Sara said before hanging up.

Carlos was soaking wet by the time he got home. He was shivering and freezing.

He pulled out a clean pair of jeans and a sweatshirt from his dresser and laid them on the bed.

 Carlos gathered up a towel. He jumped into a hot shower.

After Carlos warmed himself, he headed down to the Campus Café.

The rain had stopped by then. The sun was peeking through puffs of dark grey clouds. When Carlos spotted Alice through the large pane of glass, his heart did a little dance. Oh how he loved his wife.

Alice looked adorable as she yawned. Her pink sweater dress was hugging her curves.

A cup of Hot Coco blew stem into Alice's angelic face.

Carlos slipped his arms around his wife's waist." Hi babe." Carlos said in a super cool voice.

Alice turned around to face her husband. Alice gave Carlos a passion-filled kiss.

"Babe, I don't want you to scream all over, but I have good news." Carlos said as he pulled out a chair and sat next to his wife.

Alice's face beamed with joy." What kind of news?" She asked.

"I got a job today. It's at a gas station. This old guy named Buck hired me. He seems like an ok guy. I start in the morning." Carlos said reaching for his wife's hand.

"I am so proud of you! I knew God wouldn't fail us!" Alice said.

"I saw mom today too. She is not doing well. She is down to eighty-eight pounds. I gave the doctor permission to put the feeding tube in again. Mom spit in my face today as well." Carlos looked like he was about to cry.

"Come on honey, let's go take a walk. I am really not that hungry anyway." Alice said.

Walking outside, Carlos said," I told mom that we would visit her soon."

"Of course we will. I will bring mom some flowers. She loved them last time." Alice reaching for Carlos' hand said.

"Let's talk about something else. How was your study date with the nerd?" Carlos laughed.

"Very well." Alice replied.

Carlos rolled his eyes.

"He is a really nice guy you know. I know that but the guy hates me." Carlos replied. "Oh no, it's not Jimmy I am rolling my eyes about. Look that slime bag reporter is back trying to dig up more dirt on

Frances. Look! He has Jimmy cornered. I got to go help Jimmy." Carlos said storming off to their direction.

Carlos angrily tapped on the reporter's shoulder." Hey slime ball, I think my friend said NO COMMENT!" Carlos said in a forceful tone.

"Beat it, don't you have drugs to sell to a kid on a playground." The reporter slapped back.

Carlos balled his fists. He wanted to punch the reporter in the nose.

The whole place turned silent when Jimmy punched him instead. "I said no comment!"

The reporter feel backwards holding his bloody nose.

As the reporter regained his footing he said," I'm going to sue you! You broke my nose."

Jimmy balled his fists again. Jimmy screamed," Get the hell out of here before I give you a bloody lip also!"

The reporter ran away like a baby.

Carlos put his arm around Jimmy's shoulder saying ," Come on slugger let me buy you a burger."

Jimmy quietly followed Carlos back into the Café.

"What are you having?" Carlos turned to asked Jimmy.

Jimmy struggled to find his voice. "Um- Um, a turkey burger and a coke, if that's all right." Jimmy finally said.

"A turkey burger and a coke for my friend here, a grilled chicken salad and diet coke for my wife and I'll have a root beer and chicken salad on rye." Carlos ordered.

A young woman took the order.

Jimmy helped Carlos carry the food over to the table where Alice was sitting.

Alice looked baffled. "I thought you had dinner plans with your mom?" She said.

"Oh, mom got tied up with Frances." Jimmy replied flatly as he passed Carlos a napkin.

"Tied up with Frances?" Carlos voice echoed in a confusing matter.

"Yes, my mom is a lawyer. She is going to help Frances." Jimmy replied.

"That is awesome news! I am so happy that Frances has someone on her side. How is Frances doing?" Carlos asked after wiping his face with a napkin.

"To be honest, Frances is not doing well. Mom was afraid to leave her alone. Frances is very confused and afraid." Jimmy shared.

"I wish we could do more to help. "Alice said with tears clouding her eyes.

"Oh sweetheart, please don't cry." Carlos reached for his wife's hand." There is something we all can do."

"What?" Alice asked in a weepy voice.

Carlos took out the small pocket bible that Buck had given him." We can pray. The silent inner voice of our Soul will always lead us along the right path, the path of

Goodness and Love. We know we are on the right path when our thoughts, words, and actions reflect the goodness within our souls; when that path leads us to live a life of peace, love, and compassion.

We must learn to quiet the chatter of our egoistic minds and listen instead to the wise counsel of our Soul; our Soul guidance will consistently lead us along the rightful path of goodness.

The good road leads us to a place of lasting inner peace and happiness."

The three of them joined hands. Jimmy, the lamb laid down with Carlos, the lion.

The whole café became very still and quiet again. The most profound moment in Alice's life happened in that café. When Jew and Christian, Muslim and Buddhist bowed their heads and prayed together, as one heart, one family, one spirit for Frances.

The staff, alumni, Café workers was moved to tears as Carlos the meanest, saddest, angry young man in the entire town prayed, "Live your life authentically. Wholeheartedly. Based on Love, not fear. Knowing there are no limits or boundaries to what you can do when listening to the guidance of your inner-voice.

 Embracing every experience as a blessing whether good or bad. Stay grateful for the simple things in life and do your best to stay positive every day no matter what circumstances you face. On this day, I will recall that I am a child of God. I am one who is created out of Love. I am chosen, good, holy and have purpose…a task to perform here on Earth before I return to the Father. I deserve to be treated as a person who has value and dignity.

I will embrace Frances illness as a friend this day looking for what it is teaching me about the mystery of God and Life.

I will not allow the stigma of mental illness to defeat me this day. I will choose to have power over stigma by detaching myself from the stigma.

I will talk to someone today who will encourage me to see my goodness and holiness as a child of God. Maybe we will share a prayer together for one another.

I will look for humor and reasons to laugh and be happy. Quiet joy will be my goal.

I will read a passage from Scripture or something from a book of devotion, inspiration or spiritual reading that will encourage me to trust and hope in the power and love of God.

I will seek twenty minutes of solitude, silence, prayer this day. If my mind won't quiet down, if my thoughts keep racing, I will offer that as my prayer to God. If necessary and helpful, I will listen to soothing instrumental music or inspirational/religious music to quiet me and remind me that God is present.

I will walk outdoors marveling at a sunrise, a sunset, the song of a bird, the soothing colors of nature...the serenity of green grass, a blue sky, the softness of the pastel colored blossoms of springtime and the peaceful waters of a river, lake or stream that ripple and flow. I will remind myself that everything in nature is a reflection of the Creator and pleases the Creator just as it is and so do I just as I am.

I will delight in the knowledge that we are each created different because it is in our differences we make a more powerful and beautiful whole. We each reflect a different aspect of the mystery of Life and God. Individually and together we are a Masterpiece!

In God is my hope and my joy. I will give honor, glory and praise to God knowing and trusting what God has in store for me. We do not seek or like suffering but our suffering can make us strong in many ways and more compassionate and loving to others...our brothers and sisters in the Lord. Dear Lord, Have mercy on us, those who suffer from mental illness. Please bring us comfort during our darkest hours and free us from confusion and emptiness. Help us cling to You Lord when symptoms take over our very being. We pray that Your Holy Spirit residing deep within us awakens our hearts and minds. When we are well, may we be grateful for all the healing, you bring into our lives. Thank You for the good people you put along our path, such as family, friends, peers, and brothers and sisters in the Lord.

We also pray that society continues to respect us. We desire to be treated with dignity and free from stigma Let us be reminded that we are created in Your image Lord, and that You call us forth to a new life Keep us safe Lord, in your loving and forgiving arms. In Your Name Jesus. Amen."

The café crowd remained silent and prayerful until Carlos took a bite of his sandwich.

It was then everyone in the Café returned to its normal chatter.

Alice smiled then. "I think your cover is blown honey. Everyone knows you have a big heart now."

Carlos laughed." Well, I guess I couldn't be cool forever."

"Jimmy said," Carlos, if it is at all possible I think you are even cooler than before."

Lee Roy walked up to the table then." Hey Jimmy, Wow man, what a right hook! Who taught you to punch like that?"

Jimmy laughed." My mom. She boxed a little in Collage."

The topic quickly turned to Frances. " Yo! Carlos, you know I have been thinking, maybe we should talk to Professor Bruce about having a fundraiser for Frances. She is going to need mega bucks to pay her lawyer fees and find a place to live after this is all over."

"Hey man that's not a bad idea. Jimmy you are pretty tight with Bruce. Maybe you can talk to him about it." Carlos said.

Bruce watched as his four students sat together. Four students he never thought would be friends were now bonded by the heart.

Bruce wanted to join his students at the table and be a part of all that love be he held back.

"Oh no Frances, what have you done?" Sara asked in a desperate tone. Sara walked into a destroyed hotel room.

The T.V. was knocked off its stand. The sheets were ripped off the bed and the mirror was shattered.

A tall gentle giant of a man stood beside Sara. He turned to Sara saying," Let me handle this."

Sara backed up." Please do." She said.

The man identified himself as Dr. Turner to Frances. He took some gentle steps towards Frances.

Frances flinched in fear.

"Don't be afraid Sweetheart, I won't hurt you. I am here to help you." Turner said in a calm and silky voice.

"Make them go away!" Frances screamed as she pointed to a corner where no one stood.

"O.K. I will ask them to leave." Turner said playing along.

Turner walked over to the corner and said," Will you please leave?"

Turner then turned to face Frances." They said they are leaving." He replied.

That seemed to calm Frances quite a bit.

Just as Frances was calming down, the police arrived.

A large brick wall of a man handcuffed Frances after the hotel manager said he wanted to press charges.

"Can't I just pay for the damage? I mean you have to understand, the poor girl is ill." Sara said in a very soft tone.

The red-faced manger replied," Have you seen the room?"

The cop said," We are going to have to take her in."

Dr. Turner said to the hotel manager," May I speak to you outside for a moment?"

"Yeah, I guess." The manger replied.

Turner and the hotel manager walked outside into a large hallway that was painted red.

"Listen, I know my patient did a lot of damage but isn't there a way we can work this out?" Turner asked pulling out a stack of 100 dollar bills from his wallet.

"Maybe." The manager said as greed filled his heart.

"How do you want to be remembered...for all the great things you have or for all the great things you've done? ~Make a Difference~. Make a difference in that young lost girl's life." Turner said.

"O.K. I will drop the charges. But it's going to cost you. My time and silence is very valuable." The manager said.

Turner handed the man some money. But the manager said," This doesn't even begin to cover the damage or my silence."

By the time the manger was done hustling Turner, Turner was out nearly $3,000.

The officer unhand cuffed Frances when the manager said he wanted to drop the charges. The officer, a Christian looked relived.

"We will need to find another place to stay." Sara said to Turner as they loaded Frances into a waiting cab.

Turner looked at Sara and said," No worries. My best friend Sarah will be more than willing to put you up. Why don't I give her a call now, and let her know we are on the way."

"You're a God send. Thank you!" Said relived Sara.

Turner pulled out of his pocket a cell phone. He dialed Sarah's number.

"Hi Sarah." Turner said.

Sarah who was baking a batch of cookies wiped her hand on a dish towel. She answered the phone on the second ring.

"Hello." Sarah replied when she heard Turner's voice.

"Sarah, I have two friends here, that need a place to stay for a while. Do you think you can help them out?" Turner asked.

"Of course I can. That's what angels are for!" Sarah giggled. Turner's laugh was hardy and joyfully. So much so it made Frances laugh.

Turner thanked Sarah. He then hung up his cell phone. With cat-like moments he turned to Sara saying, "My friend Sarah is delighted to help us. Shall we go then?"

Sara's worried looked changed in that moment. Sara's face muscles relaxed. "Sure." Sara replied.

"Frances, we are going to go to my friends Sarah's house. You will like it there." Turner replied.

Frances began biting herself. Like a child she demanded," I want my mommy! I want to go home!"

Dr. Turner gently took Frances by the hand. He sat her in the back seat of his car.

"I want to go home!" Frances demanded again.

Turner buckled Frances seat belt. Frances bite him in the shoulder. Sara's mouth dropped open.

"Frances did the bad voices tell you to do that to me?" Turner softly asked.

Frances puffed out her cheeks then. She started yelling." They are mad at you! They don't like you!"

Sara slide in near to Frances. "They like her! She is nice. Men are men!" Frances said grabbing Sara's hand.

Dr. Turner slid behind the steering wheel. He buckled himself in." Frances, I'm sure they will like me when they get to know me. Why don't we play a game? Why don't you ask me a question? I'll answer it. Then I will ask you one. Then you will answer ok?"

Frances said," All-right. What is your favorite color?"

Dr. Turner replied," Red." He then asked Frances," Why don't they like men?"

"The voices don't like men because they like to hit little girls. Men are mean. Men can't be trusted." Frances replied.

"Oh, I see." Turner replied.

The game went on for many miles. By the end of the car ride, Dr. Turner had discovered that Frances had six different personalities, ranging from a two-year old child to a 100 year old man named Derick.

Dr. Turner pulled his SUV in front of a cozy looking two- story home.

In the front of the house there was a cute white picket fence, marigold gardens, a lush eternal green lawn and neatly trimmed bushes.

The house screamed," Americana."

Frances child personally came out in that moment." Oh, Pretty." She said.

A moment later Frances changed into the old man saying," The park bench was deserted as I sat down to read. Beneath the long, straggly branches of an old willow tree. Disillusioned by life with good reason to frown, for the world was intent on dragging me down. And if that weren't enough to ruin my day, a young boy out of breath approached me, all tired from play. He stood right before me with his head tilted down, and said with great excitement,

"Look what I found!" In his hand was a flower, and what a pitiful sight, with its petals all worn -- not enough rain, or too little light. Wanting him to take his dead flower and go off to play, I faked a small smile and then shifted away. But instead of retreating he sat next to my side, and placed the flower to his nose and declared with overacted surprise, "It sure smells pretty and it's beautiful, too. That's why I picked it; here, it's for you." The weed before me was dying or dead. Not vibrant of colors, orange, yellow or red. But I knew I must take it, or he might never leave. So I reached for the flower, and replied, "Just what I need."

But instead of him placing the flower in my hand, He held it mid-air without reason or plan. It was then that I noticed for the very first time that weed-toting boy could not see: he was blind. I heard my voice quiver, tears shone like the sun. As I thanked him for picking the very best one. "You're welcome," he smiled, and then ran off to play, Unaware of the impact he'd had on my day. I sat there and wondered how he managed to see. A self-pitying

Man beneath an old willow tree. How did he know of my self-indulged plight? Perhaps from his heart, he'd been blessed with true sight. Through the eyes of a blind child, at last I could see .The problem was not with the world; the problem was me.

And for all of those times I myself had been blind, I vowed to see the beauty in life, and appreciate every second that's mine. And then I held that wilted flower up to my nose, and breathed in the fragrance of a beautiful rose. And smiled as I watched that young boy, another weed in his hand, about to change the life of an unsuspecting old man."

Sara watched and observed all of Frances' personalities joining in on the conversation.

Sarah stood on the front porch of the well-groomed home. Sarah was wearing a fifties- style house dress with a white apron tied around her waist. Her long blond hair was tied up with a red ribbon.

Sliver moonlight feel against her pretty round face illumining her white smile.

A smile that embraced Frances' troubled soul like an old friend.

"She looks nice." Frances said.

"My friend Sarah is very nice. She is a friend to everyone she meets." Dr. Turner said.

Sarah greeted Turner with a hug. She introduced herself to Sara by shaking her hand.

But it was Frances that surprised them all by saying," You look like an angel. How come I can't see your wings?"

Sarah replied," Not all angels have wings. Sometimes it's their hearts that make them angelic."

Frances gave Sarah a hug. Frances' inter-child then said," Will you be my friend just like my other best friend Sara?"

Sarah replied," Of course."

Sara mouthed the words," Thank you." To both Sarah and Dr. Turner as grateful tears filled her eyes.

"Why, don't we all go inside? I made cookies. "Sarah joyfully announced.

Inside the warm and cozy house, Sarah took Frances into the kitchen. She set a tall glass of milk and a dish of cookies in front of Frances." Help yourself." Sarah said.

Frances eat the cookies and drank the milk like a two-year old learning how to fed herself. She had cookie crumbs and spilled milk everywhere, but Sarah didn't seem to mind it one bit.

Sara admired the beautifully decorated home.

Inside the living room where Sara was seated with Dr. Turner, Sara looked at the pictures on the mantle. Pictures that were mostly of Dr. Turner and happy children.

There was also a wide-picture-window dressed with handsome brown and white curtains that Sarah had hand made. There was also a writing desk, brown chairs and a large flat screen T.V.

"Would you like a tour?" Sarah asked Sara while Dr. Turner tended to cleaning up Frances.

"I would love one." Sara replied feeling a warm and tenderness towards the kind woman who shared her name.

Sarah first took Sara into her beautiful kitchen. A kitchen that shined with stainless steel cookware, stove and fridge. There was also a breakfast nook and another large window.

Next the two woman took a winding staircase up to a second floor that lead to four bedrooms. Each bedroom hosting a different theme.

One bedroom had a Raggedy Ann and Andy theme. In that room the walls were painted a bright red.

The next room was called, "The Seashell room." It had a beach theme. The walls were painted a sea blue.

The third room encompassed a garden theme. It was filled with flowers and an actual gazebo.

That was the bedroom Sara feel in love with.

The last bedroom was called "The Ranch." It was decorated with all kinds of horse and cowboy items.

Returner took the time to learn more about Frances.

Frances' old man personally revealed," You know that girl's dad used to hit her. He blamed her for her mother being a slob. He's an S.O.B. He made her do things to him too. Things only a wife should do to her husband. You don't know how much pain that caused Frances. And her mother, Oh Lord, her mother is a slob. Because she horded so much Frances had to use the bathroom outside because the bathroom was filled with junk. She had to wash up with a hose like she was a dog. And her potty was a hole in the ground. I could kill them for what they did to her."

"How often did Frances father abuse her?" Dr. Turner asked.

"That S.O.B. did it every day. Expect when she had her period. It was then when they couldn't have sex that he hit her." The old man went on to say.

It was then the little girl personally began to speak, "He was really mean. Sometimes he used to lock us in the basement. It was dark in there. And big rats."

"I bet that made Frances really mad." Dr. Turner said.

An unknown seventh personality appeared then." It did. That's when I told Frances she should kill them. Those students at the collage. The ones with the so-called happy and perfect families. They all desire to die! No one should live a perfect life. I was trying to save them from their perfect families! Frances family was supposed to be perfect too!"

Dr. Turner took notice of this very dominate personality.

"Alice! Frances was not blind to her pain. Perfect Alice was supposed to be the first to die. She was Frances best friend. Frances didn't want her to feel the pain of this world anymore. "

"What do you think killing the students would have accomplished?" Dr. Turner went on to ask.

"I was going to save them. Death would have saved them all. Now they have to go back to living with the pain of their perfect families. Don't you see no one sees what goes on behind closed doors." The unknown personally shared.

Dr. Turner could see that Frances' entire body was shaking then.

The unknown personally laughed. Then in a mock- Elvis voice said," Frances has left the building. Frances has left her mind. Frances has left this world and all its pain behind. No one will speak to Frances without speaking to me first."

"Where did Frances go?" Dr. Turner asked.

"She is playing hide and seek." The little girl personally returned then.

"Do you think if I count to ten, she will come out and talk to me?" Turner played along.

Frances' entire body shook with laugher as the little girl sing-singed," Yes. She likes to play hide-and-seek."

Dr. Turner started counting. By the time he got to ten, Frances was once again demanding to go home.

Sara and Sarah had been watching the entire conversation unfold in front of their very eyes.

"It's getting late, Perhaps I should let you get settled into your rooms." Sarah replied.

"I am beat." Sara agreed.

Sara was overjoyed that she would be staying in the garden room.

Frances seemed to be captured by the calm and magic by the horse room.

Frances actually feel asleep peacefully just moments after Sara touched her in.

Sarah and Turner sat down on the living room sofa together. They shed their earthly form. They stretched out their wings and began to glow. The two angels had known each other for centuries now.

A golden light feel around Sarah. She smiled and the entire room lit up like the Summer sun.

"I think Frances is the sweetest girl I have ever met. I give my right wing to right all the injustices that has been done to her." Sarah declared.

"I am fond of Jimmy and Carlos myself." Turner replied as his halo became a dazzling wall of white.

Sarah laughed. "I do recall an angel named Turner sitting on his cloud shaking his wing at Carlos."

Turner replied," All-right I admit it. I didn't have faith that Carlos could change, but he proved me wrong."

Sarah took a throw pillow and started a pillow fight with Turner.

Out of breath from laughing so hard, Turner said," You really are a sassy angel today aren't you?"

Sarah's cheeks were filled with a color of springtime roses as she replied," I guess I am. I feel like something amazing is going to happen. Besides, I missed you."

"Awe, I missed you too." Turner replied.

"Restless- Chapter Six"

Carlos got up at the crack of Dawn. He was surprised to see Alice already up.

"Honey, you didn't have to get up so early." Carlos said.

"Are you kidding? I wouldn't let you start your very first day of work on an empty stomach. Besides it's Easter Sunday. I want to go to the sunrise service they are holding on campus today." Alice replied.

"I understand. I am sorry, I can't go with you this morning, but last night after you feel asleep, I took a walk. I got so inspired as I was walking under the stars, I came home and wrote a poem. Would you like to hear it?" Carlos asked.

"Of course! You know how much I love your poems. They make my heart dance." Alice replied.

Sitting down together in front of dishes filled with eggs and bacon, butter rolls and cups of coffee, Carlos shared his heart," Come with me to the foot of the Cross,

Where the Son of Man redeemed our loss. A man of no import, wealth or fame, His body strewn on a wooden frame. Come with me to the foot of the Cross, Where the sin of the world as an albatross. Lie bare to the multitude for all to see, the mysteries of eternity. Come with me to the foot of the Cross, Where even his garments were sold and tossed. His cry of thirst in ear shot of all, was met, with the taste of gall.

Come with me to the foot of the Cross, A nail, the spear, in time embossed. He cries 'Forgive them for they know not what they do, the raiment being torn in two. Come with me to the foot of the cross, Questioning agony of a mother's loss. 'Mother behold your Son' he cries. The earth awash in rumbling sighs. Come with me to the foot of the Cross, The guards shout, and 'this was the Son of God.' Transforming power through the shedding blood, their hearts changed as in a raging flood. Come with me to the mountain Tomb, Where kept inside this earthly womb. The temple of the living God, Who's feet upon the earth once trod. Come with me to the mountain Tomb, A vigilant guard to be assumed.

Whose watch though long could not foresee, the earth contained eternity. Come with me to the mountain Tomb, The nightly watch of men attuned. The shock of boulder, rock and stone, Cast aside, answers unknown. Come with me to the empty Tomb, Where the Son of Man was thought to loom. All that was left were garments stained, the precious blood upon them remained. Come with me to the empty Tomb, 'He Has Arisen! 'As a flower in bloom. The memory of His promise that his Temple would be raised, Filled their hearts with joy, to God be all the praise."

"Oh Carlos, that is so beautiful. How can you not want to share your poetry with the world?" Alice said with tears in her eyes.

"I told you baby, it's too personal. All my poems are my love letter to God." Carlos replied.

"Well that was a lovely way to start off Easter Sunday." Alice said kissing her husband.

Carlos and Alice eat their breakfast. As Carlos left for work that morning feeling happy and forgiven.

Buck stood in front of a large red toolbox searching for a screwdriver. He did not know Carlos was standing behind him.

Buck searched until he found what he was looking for.

"Excuse me sir." Carlos said politely.

Buck turned around. "Oh good you are here. You are even here early. Why don't I show you where I need you to start?" Buck said in a cheery voice.

Carlos followed Buck into the office. Buck said," You can start in here. I will need you to sweep and mop, water the plants and drop this mail off for me."

"Sure, I will get right to work." Carlos said smiling. "Good." Buck replied, then walked out to the bay area of his Garage.

Carlos took care of all the tasks, Buck asked him to do. At 11 am, Carlos' stomach began to rumble. Buck took notice. "Are you hungry son? If you are, you can go to lunch."

It was then Carlos realized, he had forgotten to pack his lunch. "Oh man, I forgot to pack lunch." Carlos said snapping his fingers.

Buck smiled. He opened his desk drawer. He handed Carlos a paper bag that had in it a grape juice box and a peanut butter and jelly sandwich." I always pack an extra lunch just in case." Buck said.

"Thank you so much!" Carlos said smiling.

Buck was taking a bite of his own sandwich when he noticed a picture of Carlos on the front page of a local newspaper.

"Hey, kid did you see this?" Buck asked.

Carlos took the paper from Buck's hands. On the front page of the paper was Carlos. Carlos' eyes were closed in prayerful thought as he held Buck's bible in his hands.

The headline read," Former bad boy now a minster!"

Something about the headline sent a kind of joy into Carlos' heart. "That sounds pretty cool. Minster!" Carlos replied.

Carlos' joy turned into anger however when he began reading the article.

The article was written by the reporter, Jimmy punched. It read," Carlos, the angry teen has a long police record that includes drug activity, violence, and robbery. I don't mind saying this but this reporter would never enter this teen's church if he were a real minister for fear that I might be mugged at the alter or worse."

Then the article became even uglier as the reporter wrote," Carlos' mother is locked up in a mental asylum for non-criminal behavior as this monster walks free. Where is the justice in that? This reporter calls on the public to take back the streets from gang members like these, the ones that walk out on Sunday to do drive-by shootings and drug deals in city parks where your children play."

Carlos spit fire as he stormed out of the gas station dropping the paper on the floor.

Buck went after him, after he read what the ugly reporter wrote.

With no one else to talk to, Carlos poured out his heart to Buck.

"No, one understands what I go through with my mom. My grandfather disowned her and stopped paying for her care a long time ago. That's why I started selling drugs. I wanted my mom to have the best care possible. I wanted my wife to get a Collage education. My grandfather he donates to the Collage where my wife and I attend, he is on my back all the time. If I don't graduate he will ruin my life. He has threatened serval times to use his power to pull my wife's scholarships. That's why I sell drugs to keep my wife in school. No one helps people like me. I would never hurt a fly I have never done a drive-by shooting. I am not in a gang and I don't sell drugs to little kids. I do it to keep my mom where she needs to be so she won't die out on the lonely, mean streets and so my talented wife can have a good life. I swear I am not the monster the papers say I am."

Buck put his arm around Carlos. Buck said," I know you are in horrible pain right now. I know you feel like society and everyone has abandon you. You feel like God can't see your pain. But none of that is true, you need to reach out to people that care. There is no shame in loving a person with mental illness. There isn't any shame in making mistakes. Go out into the world Carlos and let the light of who you really are shine. There might be someone right now living in darkness, that needs your light to find their way back home. When we recognize that our personal good coincides with the Good of everyone, our inner light is turned on: at this point, when a human being becomes a Human Angel, their light, like a beacon, shines all around. Let the tears of your past be water for the flowers of your future happiness. Gratitude unlocks the fullness of life. It turns what we have into enough, and more. It turns denial into acceptance, chaos to order, confusion to clarity. It can turn a meal into a feast, a house into a home, a stranger into a friend. "Gratitude unlocks the fullness of life. It turns what we have into enough, and more. It turns denial into acceptance, chaos to order, confusion to clarity. It can turn a meal into a feast, a house into a home, a stranger into a friend. Gratitude makes sense of our past, brings peace for today, and creates a vision for tomorrow. So many of us walk the planet overwhelmed with self-hatred, our earth suits riddled with bullets forged in the fires of shame. For too many, their experience of normal includes beating themselves up for simply being human… How very sad, and deeply unnecessary. So much brilliance lives below our shame shackles… We need to honor and validate each other. We need to build the healthy ego. We need to help free each other from our shame shackles. We need to meet each other with compassion for this very difficult human journey…We need to know God Loves us. "

"Thank you Buck for listening to the cry of my soul. No one besides my sweet Alice has ever done that for me." Carlos admitted.

"Come on Kid, Let's go finish our lunch." Buck said.

Jimmy's classmates promptly took their seats in Bruce's classroom. They couldn't wait to see what Jimmy had to say next.

Even Carlos rushed back to campus from work. In spite of rival drug dealers threating him, Carlos made it back to class on time.

Jimmy took his spot in front of the class." The last time I addressed you, I spoke of how my dad met my mom. Alice asked me how my dad proposed, but before I tell you that, I must share what happened next. My grandma's health declined. She was diagnosed with cancer of the breast. The preacher, the man my grandma trusted and had grown to love could not take care of my grandma because of his own failing health in spite of his love for her.

My dad now 18 had to move the preacher into a nursing home. The preacher was losing his memory. Soon he didn't know anyone."

"What did your dad do at that moment?" Bruce asked.

"Well, after moving the preacher to a nursing home, He packed up my uncle, grandma and himself and moved to Sara's parents' house. Sara's mother was a compassionate woman who took them in with no questions asked.

My dad was living with Sara's mother for three weeks when my grandmother passed away in the middle of a balmy Summer's night.

As my mother tells it," Grandma called them into the bedroom one by one. A bed that was once my mother's. Grandma told each of them she loved them and that she would see them again in Heaven. She then took my dad's hand, kissed it and took her last breath. Mom said Dad wouldn't wash his hands for weeks after she died. My grandma was buried by her 1st husband. Grandma was finally was returned to her first and only love, God. After Grandma died, Dad feel into a dark depression. He didn't eat or sleep, he didn't shower, he began using again. He and mom broke up.

Dad once again took to the streets. It was not until another great tragic event happened that my dad returned home."

Alice bite a fingernail." What happened to make your father return?'

"Well, it was an extremely cold Winter's night when My other Grandma, Sara's mother went to the store to buy my uncle hot coco. My mother had begged her not to go out. It had been snowing all day. Mom feared there would be black ice on the road. My grandma kissed my mom saying she would be fine. Mom got a sick feeling in the pit of her stomach. Hours passed, my grandma did not return. My mom starting calling the hospitals. It was 4 am when a policeman came to the door. My mom and my uncle who had downs syndrome was given the heartbreaking news.

Grandma, had hit a patch a black ice, she had drowned in a raging river."

The class gasped at Jimmy's words.

"Your poor mom and uncle! They must have been out of their minds with sadness not knowing where your father was at that time." Bruce said.

"We were." A woman's voice echoed from the back of the classroom.

Everyone turned around to see a stunning woman standing there. She took Bruce's breath away. The woman looked like his late wife.

Jimmy introduced the woman." Everyone this is my mom Sara."

Bruce shook Sara's soft hand. He felt lighthearted and a bit dizzy as he looked into her eyes." Jimmy, it would be interesting to hear from your mom what happened next."

The class agreed. "Do you mind mom?" Jimmy asked.

"No not at all." Sara replied. Sara walked up to the head of the classroom. She was wearing a pair of pink heels, a pink sweater and grey tweed pants.

"After my mom died we hardly had enough money to bury her. Some of the church people got together and took up a collection for Alan and I. We were heartbroken even after we buried mom, Simon didn't come home. Someone had turned me into the child welfare people. They had concerns that I could not support Alan and myself. They were right. I struggled to put food on the table. Some days I didn't eat because there was not enough food for the two of us. The welfare people wanted to take Alan away from me.

One day a man came to my door. I was having a bad day. I was preparing to go to the hearing to keep Alan. The last thing I wanted anyone do is visit but something told me to answer the door. I didn't know the man at first. The man stood with his back towards me. He was tall and wearing an Army uniform.

When he turned around I couldn't believe my eyes. It was Simon. Clean, sober and in the Army. He was holding a ring in his hand. I don't even think I waited for Simon to propose to me before I shouted ," Yes!"

We ended up getting married just an hour before the hearing for Alan. I wore an old white dress of my Mothers. Simon wore his uniform. It was short of a fairy tale but romantic just the same. We exchanged Weddings band. Simon's ring was from a cracker jack box."

"Wow, that's deep that you loved each other so much." Leon said.

"Yes, it was son. After our wedding we were allowed to adopt Alan because the judge to was in the Army. We lived in my mom's house until Simon was drafted for the Vietnam War. "

"Little Alice, Is that really you?" Sara said as the bell rang.

Alice feel into the open arms of Sara. "Yes, it is me." Alice replied.

"My goodness, have you grown. Let me take a good look at you." Alice spun around.

"My, My you are so pretty." Sara said smiling.

"Oh, thank you." Alice replied smiling.

The students still seated wanted to stay after class so they could hear more of the story. Sara was happy to share. But as she was about to speak, Frances intruded her with an urgent phone call.

"I am sorry. I have to go." Sara said.

Jimmy was worried about his mother, so he followed her out into the hallway.

"Mom, wait! What's the matter?" Jimmy asked.

"Honey no time to talk. I have to go now." Sara replied.

"Wait, Mom I am going with you. You are as white as a ghost." Jimmy said.

Sara didn't argue with her son. Jimmy and Sara were not aware that Jimmy's class was following them. They too were worried.

Inside the rental car, Jimmy said," Please mom tell Bruce and I what is wrong."

Sara was shocked to see Bruce in the backseat.

Sara crying now said," I shouldn't have left Frances. It's a nightmare"

Bruce said," Breathe. Good. Breathe deeply. Now exhale."

Sara was calmer now.

"I left Frances with Dr. Turner a court appointed doctor and his friend Sarah. Dr. Turner wanted to spend time with Frances. But Turner just called me, He had taken

Frances to an ice cream shop and when he was paying for the ice cream Frances ran away." Sara shared.

"We will find her Mom." Jimmy said.

"We will stop at Sarah's house." Sara said.

Turner and Sara sprang from the porch steps. Sara quickly introduced her son and Bruce to them.

Turner asked," O.K. but who are all these other people?"

It was then Jimmy noticed his classmates standing behind them. "These are my classmates." Jimmy introduced his classmates.

Jimmy turned to his classmates saying," Frances is missing. We all need to fan out and find her."

"No! We need to call the police. Frances is confused. She could get violent if she sees all of you coming." Dr. Turner said.

"We can't call the police. They will put her in jail. We can't let that happen." Carlos said.

"Wait! I think I might know where she is." Alice spoke up then. "Can I borrow your car?" Alice asked Sara.

Sara tossed her the keys. "Oh of course." Sara said.

Dr. Turner said," I don't think this is a good idea."

"I am her best friend. I will find her." Alice said.

"We will find her." Carlos corrected his wife.

"All right. We will give you a few hours. But after that we will have to call the police." Turner said.

"Where are we going?" Carlos asked Alice.

As Alice threw the gear shift into drive and sped away , she replied, " I think Frances might be headed towards her childhood home."

"But we don't know how to get there." Carlos replied.

"I do. I went there." Alice let the cat out of the bag.

Carlos' eyes went wide with shock." You did? Why?" He said.

"I had to see it. I had to see what our best friend lived through. Carlos, it is horrible. A trash dump looks cleaner. The house should be torn down. The walls bleed with Frances' pain. It is like a haunted house that screams out." Alice said as she took a sharp right turn.

"Slow down please! The tires are burning!" Carlos said after he and his wife had been driving for an hour.

"That's not the tires." Alice replied.

"Yes, it has to be. Something stinks!" Carlos said. Alice got solely quiet then." Please don't tell me that smell is coming from the house. It smells like someone died!" Carlos said.

The little ranch house sat on a lot that looked like a trash dump. Old sofas, rotten food, dirty clothing and human waste cluttered the lawn.

"I can't believe Frances had to grow up like this. I thought I had it bad." Carlos shaking his head in horror said.

"Carlos, we won't be able to stay in that house long, so if Frances is in there, Let's get her fast. Cover your face and hose as you walk in." Alice warned her husband.

As Alice and Carlos navigated their way through the yard, Carlos felt sicken by what he saw.

Things a normal person would have treasured like family pictures, baby shoes and wedding dresses was tossed out into the yard. They were covered with dirt and dog waste.

The inside of the house was even more terrible.

Carlos could hardly see his wife over the high stacks of trash.

Alice gagged from the smell. "Frances are you in here?" She called out. Only dead silence echoed back.

Carlos called out then," Frances, if you are in here please answer."

The smell was becoming too much for the couple to bear. Carlos and Alice were about to give up their search when they her Frances say," I can't find my dolly!"

Frances sat in the middle of an overflowing litter box crying. Carlos became Frances' father in that moment. He scooped her up into his arms. He said," Come on baby, we are going to go to Toys R Us. I am going to buy you a new doll because you were such a good girl."

Frances' eyes sparkled in that moment. "A brand new Dolly?" She asked with the joy of a four-year-old.

"Of course!" Carlos said trying to hold back tears.

Frances hugged Carlos." I love you daddy!" She said. Alice couldn't help but cry.

On the way back to Sarah's house, Carlos kept his promise and bought Frances a new, her first ever Barbie Doll.

Frances was thrilled.

Alice was left sadden by the whole thing. She was very quiet and as white as a ghost on the way back to Sarah's house.

 Nearly everyone burst into tears when they heard what Carlos had done.

When Frances stepped out of the car, everyone that knew Frances had noticed the changes in her. Frances had lost a lot of weight. She looked tired and gaunt. She had lost a lot of her hair. Her entire personally was different.

Frances was no longer the bright and bubby girl her classmates and Professor had known.

Sara calmly took Frances by the hand and led her into the house.

"Thank you Alice." Sara said tearfully." Thank you Carlos." Bruce said.

Jimmy followed his mother into the house. "Are you going to be all-right mom?" Jimmy asked as concern overshadowed the light in his eyes.

"Yes, I will be now. I think you and your friends should go home now. Turner, Sarah and I need to get Frances washed up. We need to figure out what to do next." Sara said.

"Mom, I think I should just hang out here for a while. In case you need me." Jimmy said.

Turner now inside the house said," That might be a good idea. I don't mind at all."

Everyone else parted ways then after saying Good Night to one another.

Sara and Sarah washed up Frances.

"Would you like something to drink?" Dr. Turner asked Jimmy as he sat on the sofa.

"No, Thanks." Jimmy said holding up his hand.

"Do you want to talk about what happened today?" Dr. Turner asked Jimmy.

Jimmy and Dr. Turner sat down a crossed from one another.

"What happened to my friend?" Jimmy asked sadly. "She is very ill. She has many different personalities." Dr. Turner eyes filled with sorrow as he reviled that news to Jimmy.

"What will happen to her? She can't stand a trial." Jimmy said.

"The DA will not drop the charges. We just have to try to beat the charges and get the help Frances need. The sad fact is Jimmy there are more people in jail that have mental illness then there are in Hospital. The government keeps cutting down health care for those who are sick like Frances.

There is nowhere else for them to go." Dr. Turner said.

"Why does society allow this?" Jimmy wondered out loud. "I don't know son. There was a time, not so long ago when people cared for one another, scarified for each other, loved one another. Now a days all people care about is their own happiness, fat bank accounts, and power. Actions often speak much louder than words. When you love someone you have to act accordingly. They will be able to tell how you feel about them simply by the way you treat them over the long-term. You can say sorry a thousand times, or say "I love you" as much as you want, but if you're not going to prove that the things you say are true, they aren't. If you can't show it, your words are not sincere. And remember, it's not so much about how much you do for your loved ones as it is about the love you put into what you do for them. Learn what matters most to them and make a habit of it."

Jimmy sighed loudly." I wonder why God allows all this too. All the injustices that happen in this world."

" Well, Jimmy, God gave us free will so we can learn from the choices we make. God, knows people will make mistakes. The miracles come when we actually learn from the mistakes we make. We are meant to create a powerful movement in life. We are each given our gifts to share them with the world. We are here to create powerful waves to move obstacles within ourselves, and the entire world. Each of us has the inner power to manifest our personal dream life, and a dream world of peace, harmony & balance. By using your unique gifts, you can bring incredible movement to all, discovering or uncovering your authenticity. Our core authenticity is Love. Love encompasses peace, harmony, balance, joy, light, kindness, compassion and more. Being and sharing our internal authenticity brings the higher vibrations of Love to others, which is returned to us. Shedding everything which hides your light, the light of your soul enables you to use your unique gifts to create a powerful movement, positively impacting and changing the world." Turner replied.

" I just really hope Frances finds the kind of peace that surpasses all understanding, just like the bible talks about." Jimmy commented.

"Would you excuse me for a moment? I just want to check on Frances." Dr. Turner said.

"Unforgettable- Chapter Seven"

"Sure." Jimmy replied. Jimmy sat silently on the sofa. As Dr. Turner walked up the stairs.

"Sarah, Sara, Frances?" Dr. Turner called out.

"Call 911." Sarah cried out.

"Why?" Dr. Turner asked as he stood in the hallway near the bedroom the women were in.

"Frances, is having a miscarriage." Sarah cried.

Dr. Turner ran down the stairs and raced to the phone. Jimmy popped up from the sofa. "What is the matter?" Jimmy asked.

"Frances is having a miscarriage." Dr. Turner said as he dialed 911.

Jimmy ran up the stairs." Mom, where is Frances?" He said in a calm voice." She's in the bedroom. But please Jimmy wait downstairs." Sara replied.

Jimmy ignored his mother's orders. He pushed his way into the bedroom. Jimmy made his way over to Frances. Jimmy cradled Frances' head in his lap. "It's going to be all-right. God is holding the baby now. And from the ashes of your past, there is beauty. That is what I see in you today, and as God works "to bestow on them a crown of beauty instead of ashes, the oil of joy instead of mourning, and a garment of praise instead of a spirit of despair" , there is hope beyond measure. Frances your baby is going to have wings just like an angel." Jimmy said.

Frances balled her fists in pain. Frances' small frame shook with fear. "It hurts!" Frances screamed.

Jimmy then began singing a Richard Marx song called," Angel's Lullaby." "I was never alive. 'Till the day I was blessed with you. When I hold you late at night, I know what I was put here to do. I turn off the world and listen to you sigh, And I will sing my Angel's Lullaby."

Sara, Sarah and Dr. Turner stood in awe because Jimmy was the only one to calm Frances' troubled soul.

The paramedics arrived. When Frances saw the paramedics he old man personally cursed them saying," You are all angels of death, doom and gloom. You will never take me alive!"

The paramedics had to strap Frances down in order to bring her to the hospital.

For hours, Jimmy, his mother, Sarah and Dr. Turner awaited news on Frances. When the news came, it was not what the group had expected.

A man in his forties walked into the waiting room wearing a white uniform. He was heavy set but had a kind smile.

"Who is responsible for Frances Chung?" The man asked.

Sara jumped up." I am." She replied. "Are you her mother?" The doctor asked. Something inside Sara drove her to say," Yes, I am Frances' mother."

"Well, we saved your granddaughter and daughter. Your daughter will need to stay on bedrest for the rest of the pregnancy." The doctor replied.

Everyone let out a sigh of relief.

Jimmy asked the doctor," Can I see my sister?"

"Your sister has been through a lot today son. I think it's best that you go home for the night and see her in the morning. I am assuming your Mom will be staying with her." The doctor replied.

"Yes, I will be." Sara stated.

Dr. Turner then spoke." Doctor, I am sure you are aware that Frances has some special needs. I would like to take a few moments to go over her care with you."

The medical doctor said," I think that will be a good idea. Is her lawyer, I mean mother coming with us?"

Sara, Dr. Turner and the medical doctor walked down a hallway to an open office.

The medical doctor directed Dr. Turner and Sara to have a seat.

The medical doctor said," I am quite aware of Frances' needs. But I am not sure how we will work around the paperwork of it all, since you are not actually Frances' mother."

Sara surprised everyone by pulling a stack of papers from her oversized pocketbook." Well, I am not officially "her mother" but I am her legal guardian. Yesterday her adoptive parents signed away their rights to Frances over to me. I am in the process of adopting her." Sara shared.

The medical doctor glanced over the papers Sara handed over to him." Well, that makes my job a whole lot easier then." He said.

Dr. Turner asked Sara," Does Jimmy know?"

Sara said," No, I haven't gotten a chance to talk to him alone yet, but I am sure he will support me on this. After all who else does Frances have now?"

Carlos and Alice sat with Raina as Raina counted every bloom on the flowers, Alice gave to her.

When Raina was done counting the blooms, a small moment of sanity came over Raina." I read the paper today. I saw the story that mean reporter wrote on us son. I wanted to tear that guy to pieces."

"Mom, I know it hurt you to see that, but it is better that it's out in the open. A good friend of mine told me that maybe our story will help others. There is no shame in having a mental illness. And I know that what the reporter wrote about me isn't true, and the ones that love us know it too." Carlos shared.

"Carlos, I want you to listen to me. There is a new drug out on the market called," Prozac." It's supposed to help people like me. I want you to give the doctor permission to give it to me. I want to get better." Raina said.

After Raina said this, she slipped back into a confused state of mind.

'Prozac, I never heard of that before. Have you?" Alice said to her husband.

"Oh, yes dear I have. I have actually done some research on the drug. Some people do get better, but the side effects concern me." Carlos replied.

"Side effects. What kind?" Alice asked.

"Anxiety, nervousness, nausea, rash, pruritus, insomnia, asthenia, and headache." Carlos replied.

"Mom, Looks tired. Why don't we talk about this at home?" Alice suggested.

Carlos kissed his mom. Alice followed. "Goodbye Mom, We will see you next week." Alice said.

Raina did not reply.

Bruce needed to take a walk. He needed to breathe in the cold night air. He needed to hide his sadness in the shadows and talk to God.

Bruce walked out his office. He found himself walking down a lonely sidewalk- thoughts swirled around his mind like a tidal wave in a vase blue ocean.

Bruce thought about his wife and his child- after receiving the phone call from Jimmy that Frances was a mom-to-be.

Bruce wondered what he could do to help Frances and her unborn child. Bruce found himself in front of a local eatery called," Heart and Soul."

Bruce thought maybe a good old fashioned cup of black coffee might pick him up- so he walked inside.

Bruce was surprised to see Sara sitting alone drinking coffee and pouring over legal documents.

Walking over to Sara, Bruce asked," Is this seat taken?" He surprised Sara by the look on her face.

"I thought I was the only night owl in town. Please sit." Sara replied. "Thanks." Bruce replied.

"How was Frances when you left the hospital?" Bruce asked.

Sara looked up at Bruce with sad and tried eyes. "The doctor said she will make it, but how is Frances going to raise a child?"

"Maybe someone will adopt the baby?" Bruce suggested.

"I think I have taken on more than I can chew. I am in the process of adopting Frances, but I never thought I would be raising a baby too. Who will adopt her baby? Frances has been all over the news. She has been made a laughing stock. My main focus was to get Frances a fair trial, but now this has popped up. I just don't know what I am going to do. I can't take care of Frances plus a baby all on my own. I can't ask Jimmy to move back home. If my Simon were here he would know what to do." Sara replied.

"It is not only that we see the best in all situations, conditions, and circumstances; we must also look deeply into these things to find the true lessons and potential that they bring us. It is that we learn, grow, and fully utilize the blessings these situations, conditions, and circumstances bring us - it is that we become more than we were. This is to cultivate the true potential and blessings - to cultivate the seeds - that are within these things. In this, we will no longer see things as misfortunes; for we will know and only see them for what they truly are - Blessings of Love. When one can do this, they will find peace, and understanding in their "perceived misfortunes" in life... Do you mind if I ask you what happened to Simon?" Bruce asked.

Sara's face suddenly lit up." I don't mind at all. Now I can't give away too much because Jimmy will want to share that with you but Let's just say he died a hero in more ways than one. Tell me Bruce have you ever been so in love that their breath becomes yours?" Sara asked.

Bruce tapped his fingers against his coffee mug," Yes once. My wife died when she was very young. She was-" Bruce stopped talking, he wanted to share his heart with Sara but became overwhelmed with grief.

Sara reached for Bruce's hand." Your wife was carrying a child when she died wasn't she?"

Bruce's secret pain spilled out into his voice." Yes, she was. It was my only chance to be a dad but they both died."

"Oh, Bruce, I am so very sorry. I know it's painful Bruce, but I also know God has a plan for us all." Sara said.

"I know. I try to remind myself every day that God is in control." Bruce replied.

"You may meet someone and fall in love again." Sara said.

"I don't know about that. I haven't dated anyone since…" Bruce shared.

"I understand. I haven't dated anyone since Simon passed. I don't know if I will ever met someone that I will love as much as I loved Simon."

Bruce raised his coffee mug, "Well, Here's to God being our soulmates then." Bruce said.

Sara toasted with Bruce. The two of them spent hours talking. Sara found herself surprised that Bruce had a lot of the same qualities as Simon. He told funny jokes, was respectful and well-traveled and loved his students.

Sara also reminded Bruce of his late wife. She was pretty, soft-spoken and a gentle heart.

Buck was really impressed with Carlos. So much so he called Carlos into his office.

"Take a seat Carlos." Buck said. A nerves look spread across Carlos' face. "Did I do something wrong?" Carlos asked in a kind voice.

"Oh No! Not at all. I called you in here son because I wanted to tell you, you are doing a great job. I actually have a business proposal for you." Buck said as he leaned over on his desk.

"A proposal? Now I am intrigued. Tell me more." Carlos smiled.

"Well, I will be Frank, I am getting old. I can't keep running this place by myself anymore. I need young blood to supply new ideas, to reconnect this place to the town. I would like you to be my swing man. My assistant manager and a partner. What do you say?" Buck asked.

Carlos' eyes were filled with excitement." Really? You are not pulling my chain are you?"

"Yes, Really. You have done a fine job around here. Of course there is one condition." Buck said.

"What is the condition?" Carlos asked.

"I will give you the job and make you my partner only after you finish Collage. For now you will work part-time, learn the business from the inside. You and your wife will take the apartment around back. I will sell you half of my bossiness for what I pay for it back in the 1950s. That is $2,500. And don't worry son about giving me the money up front, I will take it out of your pay. Let's say $50.00 a week until you're paid up." Buck said.

Carlos shook Buck's hand wildly." Thank you so much sir! I will never forget this day! The day I met God through you! I will always remember for as long as I live what you have done for Alice and I!"

"Come on son, Let me show you the apartment." Buck said.

The apartment was not much to look at but Carlos was very excited about it.

The apartment was fully furnished but nothing matched. In the small Living Room was a dusty blue colored love seat. A bright orange chair, two tan tables and a black and white T.V.

The bedroom looked like a rainbow threw up. There was pink walls, a yellow bedroom set and a green rug.

The kitchen was red, it held a brown table with mismatched chairs.

The bathroom was green in color. The apartment was outdated, old and smelled like moth balls, but Carlos loved it.

As Carlos and Buck walked back to the office, Buck tossed him the apartment keys. Carlos face lit up." Thanks again Buck." He said.

"Sure, anytime. Now let's get back to work." Buck said smiling.

"Jimmy, we are all very anxious to hear what happened to your dad after he got drafted." Bruce said yawning.

"Something truly amazing happened!" Jimmy replied with his eyes sparkling with love.

"Dad, was terrified, I mean truly terrified to go to war. My mom describe it like this," On the day my dad was supposed to go to war, Dad stood at the bus-stop crying as he was saying goodbye to Alan and my mom. Dad was shaking and vomiting all over. He truly believed he was never going to see my mom again.

Mom, stood at the bus stop trying to reassure Dad that God was going to watch over him, that angels would shelter him in their wings and that she and my uncle would be fine.

Before Dad got drafted they moved to Military housing in New York City. Mom had become friends with a lot of the wives. Everyone loved Uncle Alan. When dad feel apart, mom became his rock.

Dad got on the bus not knowing if he would ever see my mom, his soulmate again. He never knew God would be so merciful to place dad's long lost friend on the bus!"

"You mean Frenchie was on the bus?" Leon asked.

"Yes! When dad saw Frenchie he thought he was dreaming! Dad began crying. Frenchie looked older. He had grown into a fine young man. Frenchie had just enlisted.

Frenchie stopped dead in his tracks. "Simon is that really you?" He questioned as he and my dad openly weep.

Dad wrapped his arms around him. Frenchie kissed him on the cheek. "I thought you were dead." My dad honestly stated.

"I almost was." Frenchie replied." After I was kidnapped. I endured many months of brutal beatings. The kidnappers locked me in a basement in chains. They denied me food and water. They told me they had killed you." Frenchie slowly reviled the details.

"Oh, Lord! How did you live through it?" Dad asked. The bus feel silent as many of the men got emotional as Frenchie replied," Faith, Brother. Faith in finding you again. Faith in God. Faith in angels. Faith in human–kind. I know that sounds crazy but because you stood up for a poor black boy, I knew not all people were bad."

"My dad once again could not control his crying." Jimmy said.

Frenchie reviled "One night the man guarding me got drunk. He feel asleep. For some reason that night I was left unchained. I was able to free myself and escape. I ran into the night. I ran and ran until I couldn't breathe. I got lost. I didn't know where I was. I tripped on something. I busted my head wide open. But that's when the real miracle happened. With blood running down my face and into my eyes, an angel came to me. She was beautiful. I mean it. She made me feel safe and loved. Wrapping her wings around me, she whispered words of peace.

The next day I woke up in a hospital. It was there I met Sister Angelica. She was a woman in her late sixties. She was very sweet, kind and loving. She had a red cherub face and gentle eyes.

Mother Angelica, a nun ran an orphanage called," House of Hope."

After I was released from the hospital, the nun took me in. She treated me like the son she never had. She loved me, I loved her.

When I told her about you, she tried to help me find you. She tried right up until the day she died.

After she died, I was 21 but I stayed at Hope House as a handy man but then the world changed. I know I had to join the Army to defend the country I loved, So here I am." Frenchie shared.

"Did Frenchie ever forgive the men that kidnapped him?" Carlos asked.

"Yes. He did. But it took him a long time too." Jimmy replied.

"My dad just couldn't believe that his best friend was sitting next to home again." Jimmy shared.

"Sunshine- Chapter Eight"

Jimmy took a moment to look around the classroom. He then said," The one thing I learned for my dad is that friendship is as rare as blue diamonds. If you find true friends you have to hold onto them and never let them go!"

Choking back tears he added," I am really glad you are my friends."

Carlos got up from his seat then. He walked up to the front of the classroom." Jimbo, we are really glad you are part of our life too." He then offered Jimmy a hug.

It was a moment of sheer joy.

Later on that afternoon, Carlos shared the news of his promotion and the apartment with Alice. Alice was thrilled.

But for some odd reason the talk between them turned from talking about wallpaper to Alice's mother.

"I should confront my mother." Alice blurred out.

"Confront your mom? What do you mean honey?" Carlos asked.

"I mean we should do an Intervention. I have never told my mom how her drinking affected my life because I was always to afraid too. Maybe now that my family's dirty little secret is out in the open thanks to that slime ball reporter, I should tell my mom how I feel." Alice said.

"Whatever you choose to do I will support you. I am sure Jimmy and his mom will too." Carlos said wrapping his arm around Alice.

Dr. Turner and Sara meet with the New Milford, C.T. district attorney. They were trying to convince him to drop the charges against Frances.

Even after Dr. Turner presented him with overwhelming proof that Frances was sexually and physically abused and that she had a true mental illness the old crow of a man would not budge on dropping or even reducing the charges.

The mean bulldog D.A. was indeed out for blood. His granddaughter had been killed in the attacks at the Columbine High School massacre. A event that changed his once gentle heart forever.

"The charges will not be dropped! That girl could have killed many innocent people!" The grumpy man said.

"Please be reasonable, Frances needs a hospital not a jail." Sara pleaded.

"Now if you don't mind, I have work to do. You have taken up enough of my time." The D.A. said.

Dr. Turner and Sara left the man's office feeling defeated and sad.

"Dr. Turner is there a church nearby? I really need some time with the Lord." Sara said.

"Sure. There is one down the road." Dr. Turner replied.

"Dr. Turner are you a believer?" Sara asked.

"He was hated and rejected; his life was filled with sorrow and terrible suffering. No one wanted to look at him. We despised him and said, 'He is a nobody!' He suffered and endured great pain for us, but we thought his suffering was punishment from God." This is the wonder of the incarnation and crucifixion. God loves us so much that he submitted himself to the depth of human pain just so he could identify completely with his children. And for us, we know that whenever we approach God in prayer, he understands fully our fears and doubt. Yes, Dear Sara, I am." Dr. Turner replied.

Dr. Turner drove to the church. From the parking lot, Sara felt drawn to the beautiful Catholic Church even though she was of a different faith.

The Church was breath-taking. It looked like a welcoming round doom from the outside. But inside it was stunning. It had lovely stained glass windows. It had a marble and stone alter. The wood floors gleamed.

Sara and Dr. Turner quietly entered the church. Sara made the sign of the cross using Holy water as she entered because she saw Dr. Turner do that.

Dr. Turner walked over to were a group of lit candles sat under a lovely statue of the Blessed Mother.

Dr. Turner himself lit a candle. He then folded his hands in prayer.

Sara slipped into a pew. She closed her eyes and began to pray.

"Lord, you are the counselor of law and statesman of integrity, merry martyr and most human of saints: Pray that, for the glory of God and in the pursuit of His justice, I may be trustworthy with confidences, keen in study, accurate in analysis, correct in conclusion, able in argument, loyal to clients, honest with all, courteous to adversaries, ever attentive to conscience. Sit with me at my desk and listen with me to my clients' tales. Read with me in my library and stand always beside me so that today I shall not, to win a point, lose my soul.

Pray that my family may find in me what yours found in you: friendship and courage, cheerfulness and charity, diligence in duties, counsel in adversity, patience in pain—their good servant, and God's first. Amen."

As Turner was praying he felt someone tap him on the shoulder.

Turner turned around to see his dear old friend and fellow angel Grandpa Miller disguised as an old priest . Grandpa Miller's friend Sarah was one of the very first humans he helped as an angel.

"It's so good to see you Grandpa. But didn't God have you on another assignment?" Turner spoke in a soft low tone so Sara couldn't hear.

"He did, but he thought you and Sarah could use some help on this one." Fr. Miller replied.

Sara walked over to where the two men were standing." Hello." Sara said to the kind-looking priest.

"Sara, this is my friend. Father Miller. Father Miller this is my friend Sara Winter." Dr. Turner introduced.

Father Miller held out his hand. Sara shook it." Pleased to meet you Father." Sara said.

"Father, can we buy you a cup of coffee?" Dr. Turner asked.

"Sure, I know the best place in town!" The old priest laughed.

Sara found herself sitting in the rectory eating butter cookies, drinking coffee and spilling out her heart.

"I don't know what to do father. I have never been so worried about a case before. I feel like God hand-picked me for this case but I don't know why. I never thought when I started the adoption process I would be adopting two children!" Sara shared.

"We might not know what the future holds but we know who is holding us. We must trust in God. He knows what is best." Father Miller offered.

"I know you are right, but I never felt so under pressure. I all-ready had one son I am raising by myself." Sara once again shared.

"God, know the worries of your heart Sara. You are not alone in all this." The kind priest spoke.

Sara glanced out the window behind Father Miller, Sara sighed." I just wish I knew what God was preparing me for."

After his last class for the day, Bruce stopped by the florist to pick up some flowers for Frances.

He picked out a breathtaking bouquet of roses. Bruce then drove over to the hospital.

Bruce's heart broke when he saw Frances. Frances looked so small lying in the bed.

"Frances, these are for you." Bruce said, as he handed Frances the flowers.

Frances, old man personality emerged. "Frances, is not here at the moment. I will make sure she gets these flowers. But I will tell you Bruce the kid is scared. She doesn't want to have a baby in Jail. She thinks everyone hates her."

"She is going to beat the charges. She has the best lawyer in the country." Bruce proclaimed.

"Hell, man wake up. Everyone already has her labeled as a nut. No matter if she is locked behind bars or locked up in her own mind, she will always be in jail." The old man said.

Suddenly Frances turned into the snot-nose, smart –mouth teenager." That old man doesn't know what he is talking about. He is bat-shit crazy. Your right Bruce she will beat the charges. But having a kid on the other hand might drive her to her grave. Frances doesn't want to be strapped down with no crying kid. She wants to party and have fun."

"What about the father? Can the father take care of the baby?" Bruce asked.

The teenage personally got very angry then." You are a nosey bastard aren't you? No, the father can't take care of the baby!"

"Why can't he?" Bruce pressed for an answer.

"Because you dummy, Frances doesn't know who the father is. She slept around you know! I told her not too, but Frances thinks that if she gives a man her body, he will love her forever. He's -" The personally broke off.

"If you know who the father is, please tell me. Like yourself, I also want to protect and help Frances." Bruce said.

Frances looked Bruce up and down." How do I know you will do right by Frances?" The teenager asked.

"Everyone can trust me. I want to help Frances just like all of you." Bruce replied.

Frances personalities all began speaking with each other.

The old man said to the teenager," I think Frances would be pissed if we told him who the father is."

The teenage personality replied," No, I think we can trust him. He looks like a good guy."

After a few moments the old man imaged." All right, I will tell you but you are not going to like what I have to say. The father drugged Frances BUT he didn't mean too. It was a complete accident. About four months ago, Leon and Carlos wanted to mess with Jimmy. One night they ran into Jimmy at a coffee bar. When Jimmy was not looking, they slipped a date rape drug into his coffee. They never knew that Frances would also end up drinking out of the same cup."

The teenager then shared," It was a cold, rainy, foggy and awful night. Frances came into the bar dripping wet. Jimmy being the good friend he was offered Frances a sip of his coffee. Because Frances was so cold she took the offer.

The next morning Jimmy woke up with Frances in his bed. I disguised myself as

Frances. Jimmy never knew he was talking to me. I lied, I told Jimmy we both got food poisoning. And that I was too sick to leave his room. He believed me. Because of the side effects of the drugs, Jimmy was feeling sick. He has no idea he is the father, neither does Frances."

"How do you know Leon and Carlos drugged Jimmy?" Bruce asked, floored by the news that Jimmy was the father.

"The old man and the little girl overheard them talking about it." The teenager replied.

"Shit!" Bruce replied.

"Oh, that man just said a bad word!" The little girl personally said.

"You have to help Frances recall what happened, so we can all help her." Bruce said addressing the teenager/old man personalities.

A nurse walked into the room then saying," I am sorry, visiting hours are over. Frances needs her rest."

Bruce's legs felt like jello as he walked out of the room. How would he tell Sara that her son was about to become a father? Could it all be just something Frances made up?

Bruce prayed over and over as he drove to meet Sara at a local café.

Leon tapped a pen against a note pad. The secret that he had been keeping was eating him up inside. Leon had to tell someone.

Leon scribed down a note and left it in Bruce's mailbox.

Leon then headed to the bus station. Leon was headed to Ohio.

Sara jumped up from her chair. "I'm sorry." Bruce said as he handed Sara his napkin.

Sara's blue silk blouse was soaking wet from the ice tea, Bruce had just spilled.

"I am so sorry. I will pay to have it dry cleaned." Bruce said, as heat rushed to his cheeks.

"It's ok really." Sara said as she dabbed her blouse with the napkin. "You are so jumpy tonight. Are you ok Bruce?"

"I just think, I am coming down with a cold."
Bruce's white lie seemed to satisfy
question.

"Maybe, we should take a rain check then. I
mean don't get me wrong Bruce, I do
like the company, but if you are not
feeling good you should rest." Sara
replied.

"Are you sure you will be ok?" Bruce asked.

"Sure, I will be. I have a lot of work to do
anyway. So a rain check would be best."
Sara replied.

"At least let me pay for your dinner." Bruce
said taking out a crisp 20$ bill.

"That is so nice of you. Thank you." Sara
replied.

"Rain check then?" Bruce asked.

"Sure." Sara said.

Sara's heart skipped a few beats as she watched Bruce walk away.

Sara thought Bruce was very handsome. He took her breath away.

Sara slapped her head with the palm of her hand. "Oh Boy, I am in trouble! That man gets my head spinning. I have my hands to full to even think about dating!" Sara berated herself.

Bruce left the eatery feeling ashamed and restless. Bruce found himself heading towards church.

 Father Miller was filling up the bulletin holder for Sunday's Mass, when Bruce strolled in.

Bruce looked like he had lost his best friend, when he gave the old priest a half-hearted wave.

Father Miller waited until Bruce had spent some time with God, before he walked over to him.

"Son, are you Ok? You look like you have a heavy burden on your heart." The old priest said.

"I am not Catholic Father." Bruce said. "I don't know what drew me here. My late wife used to come to this church but I never attended."

"Son, it doesn't matter what faith you are. All are welcomed into the Lord's house. We are all on this earth to help one another." Father Miller smiled.

"It's so complex Father. Someone told me something that could or could not be true. If it is true I will ruin many people. I just don't know what to do." Bruce reviled.

Sitting down in the pew next to Bruce, Father Miller said," I think the first thing you need to do is to take it to the Lord in prayer. Pray for guidance, wisdom and understanding. Then if it is true, you can help whoever is dealing with the issues. You don't have to have all the answers. You just have to support, love and pray for that person. Do you understand son?"

"I think so but I am not sure how to be there for them." Bruce replied.

"Just be a friend. Just love and care for them as you have done before." Fr. Miller said." Son don't you know that the miracle is not having a million friends to show off to the world. The miracle is having one friend when millions are against you. Let your prayer be "Thank You." Just keep being grateful and saying thank you every day. Don't explain, don't complain, a simple genuine thank you is enough. Be Thankful every day for your existence and you will receive more to be grateful for.

Truly the more we complain about, the more we will receive to complain about... So think with Love and not Fear to improve your life. The more we believe in Beauty within, the more beautiful our lives become. Seeing the beauty in all things is feeding our Soul daily and helping it to shine with Love. The more we focus on ugliness and fear, then our lives will become more and more in line with these things. We may not be able to change the world, but we can change OUR Inner and Outer World which helps everyone. The Lord wants us to depend on him when we don't have the answers."

Bruce smiled then. My beautiful late wife used to say, "I have cast my anchor in the port of peace, knowing that the present and future are in nail-pierced hands."

"She sounds like a smart cookie." Fr. Miller replied.

"That she was. Thank you Father, I feel so much better now." Bruce replied.

"Maybe we will see you around sometime." Fr. Miller said as he got up from the pew.

"Sure, maybe. My name is Bruce by the way." Bruce said shaking the old priest weather-beaten hands.

"Father Miller."

Father Miller watched Bruce leave the church then.

As Bruce got into his car, He asked God to guide his steps.

As Bruce was pulling away from the Church, he saw a shooting star. He knew then somehow it would all work out.

"Changes- Chapter Nine"

Bruce was shocked and horrified the next morning as he opened the mailbox. He found the note written by Leon. It read; " Dear Bruce, I know this letter is going to leave everyone baffled, but I have to leave for a while. I am leaving to try to find my father. I know this doesn't make sense now, But I think he may have information that might help Frances. Please trust me. And please keep Carlos in line. He is my best friend after all. Leon."

Bruce's legs felt weak and wobbly. He slide down to the floor, leaning his back up against the wall.

"Dear God, Please help us all." Bruce prayed.

After peeling himself from the floor, Bruce called Sara. On the phone, Bruce floored Sara by sharing the news of Leon's letter.

"Can we meet somewhere?" Sara asked.

"How about after my classes we met at the campus café?" Bruce suggested.

"Ok. Let's make it 10:15 am, I am going to go check on Frances first. Jury selection will be starting soon. I still don't know if I will put Frances on the stand or not." Sara replied.

"Ok, fine. I will see you then." Bruce said before hanging up.

At the Hospital, Frances was throwing her breakfast tray at a kind candy striper because she offered Frances a book to read. The book was Romeo and Juliet. The same book Frances' father used to read to her after he forced her to have sex.

Sara walked into the room in the middle of the chaos.

"What's going on in here?" Sara asked.

"That crazy child threw her food at me all because I offered her a book!" The woman replied.

"Frances, did you do that?" Sara asked.

"Yeah, so! She was bugging me. She gave me a bad book." Frances' little girl personally said.

Sara turned to the woman who was covered in oatmeal." I'm so sorry." Sara said." She doesn't know any better."

"Forget it." The woman said before leaving the room.

"Frances, honey. You can't be mean to people." Sara said.

The old man personally emerged then." Sara, you seem like a nice young woman. I know you are trying to help Frances. Please sit down. There is something you should know."

Sara pulled up a chair close to Frances' bed. "What would you like to talk about?" Sara asked.

Sara watched Frances take a deep breath. She then closed her eyes. When Frances opened her eyes, the teenager personally took over.

The teen spilled the beans about the night Carlos and Leon played a trick on Jimmy.

Sara's mouth dropped open. Sara tried to read Frances' facial expressions.

"I swear it's all true. Ask the old man." The teenager said.

"I don't believe you!" Sara got up for the chair and stormed out of the room.

Bruce broke the news to his dwindling class about Leon. He then asked Jimmy to try to lighten the mood by sharing his father's story.

Jimmy began with," My dad and Frenchie found themselves fighting for their life in the juggles of Nam. Dad rescued Frenchie from Death's grip many times. And to be honest Frenchie did the same for my dad.

Meanwhile, back in the States, one afternoon my mom was sitting in a doctor's office flipping through old newspapers. A young nurse with a big bright smile, took mom back into a small exam room in the Public Health Office. She made mom change into one of those thin gowns. Mom then was directed by the nurse to leave a urine sample in the bathroom.

A few moments later, an older man told mom she was pregnant with my TWIN sister and I. Mom was thrilled.

She was overjoyed, to tell you the truth she was a little scared too. She also felt in a strange way abandoned by my dad.

My dad was doing his 3rd tour in Nam. Dad was a war hero that is true, but some say mom was the real hero.

During my dad's second tour, Mom started Law School, raised her brother-in-law and went through regency without hardly any support at all.

After my mom's doctor visit, mom went back to her house to write a letter to my father.

The letter read." Dear Daddy, I do not have a face to see, or put inside a frame. I do not have soft cheeks to kiss. I don't yet have a name. Not yet can you hold my tiny hands,

Nor whisper in my ear. It's still too soon to sing a song, or cuddle me so near.

But all that will change come this October; when they say I am due. I am your baby to be; and I can't wait until I meet you! All I ask between now and then is your love for me to grow. I promise I'll be worth the wait; Just think of all the joy we'll know! So as you're waiting patiently, Please pray lots of prayers for me. I cannot wait to be a part of this wonderful family! I love you bunches and mommy too. Mommy waits by the window always looking for you!"

The class became very silent then. Bruce fought back tears as he dreamed of his own child he never got to hold.

My dad was so overjoyed that the next letter my mom got from him contained a teddy bear and some other baby items.

My mom was eight months along when she came home one day from Law School to find two solders sitting on the door step. Mom's heart stopped beating when she saw how grim their faces were.

One of the young solders, a Chaplin reviled the horrible news that my dad was taken as a P.O.W.

Mom broke down. The Chaplin had to rush mom to the Hospital. Mom delivered me without compactions. My sister Angel Rose didn't make it. My baby sister, my twin had blond hair and blue eyes.

All alone without her husband and a brother-in-law that couldn't help Mom faced the pain of losing her daughter alone.

The church my mom attended and the other Military wives all pitched in to bury my sister.

Mom moved out of N.Y. because she just couldn't be there without my dad.

She moved onto the military base in the town she grew up in. The townsfolk supplied my mom with whatever she needed. Food, clothing, paid her rent, helped take care of me and my uncle. They tied yellow ribbons around the trees in town for my dad and held prayer meetings to pray for his safe return.

Mom did the best she could. She graduated Law School. She raised my uncle and took care of her new baby.

To the outside world she looked like a strong woman but inside she was drowning.

My mom- the super woman thought I and my uncle would be better somewhere else.

So she dropped us off at a church members house, kissed us goodbye and then went back to her home. She was planning on killing herself.

She took pills from the bathroom cabinet. Mom was pouring a glass of water when she saw this blinding white light shining. It was an angel! Suddenly my mom heard me crying for her even though I was miles away! In that moment mom snapped out of her grief." Jimmy shared.

Jimmy looked around the classroom. Even tough guy Carlos was openly weeping.

"Wow, Jimmy I never knew you had a twin sister. How did your mom get through all the pain?" Alice asked.

"Mom, fully relied on her faith. She prayed daily. She talked to her guardian angels." Jimmy replied.

"It was on my fourth birthday that mom got the call that my dad, along with Frenchie and two others had been liberated from the camps.

Mom was in the middle of cutting my cake when she heard the news. She spent the entire day crying tears of joy.

The next day, Dad, Frenchie and the other men were flown to a Hospital in Paris.

All of them were in bad shape. But dad was the worst. He only weight 80 pounds, had broken ribs, a broken nose and could hardly open his eyes because he had been so badly beaten.

None of the family members of the men were allowed to see them until weeks later. Mom had contact with dad through phone calls and letters.

I was four years old when I finally heard my dad's voice for the first time.

When dad and Frenchie was to come home, the town went all out.

The Mayor declared a special Military Day honoring all the solders of our town for both past and present.

The town's people put on a parade.

Framers decorated their tractors with white, red and blue ribbons and flags.

Main Street was decorated with red and blue lights.

All the store fronts were dressed in red bows and flags. It looked like the Fourth of July.

There were hot dog vendors, ice cream and balloons for the kids.

Dad and Frenchie had a hero's welcome.

The thing was Dad and Frenchie did not return as the same men. The war had changed them.

Frenchie ended up becoming mentally ill. He had nightmares, blackouts, and periods he couldn't recall his own name. Frenchie was in and out of the Hospital.

My dad became withdrawn and angry. He hurt for the men that came home that did not have a hero's welcome. My dad was combative at times, thinking he was still in the war.

Dad always had sadness in his eyes. He was very quiet. He never talked about what happened to him. He couldn't connect to mom and I, the only person he could relate to was Frenchie.

This went on for months. I was turning five and had never once gotten a hug from my father.

Then one day something happened. My uncle was struggling to plant some flowers. Seeing his brother's sadness, my dad walked over to my uncle. Dad knelt down next to my uncle. Dad showed my uncle how to plant the flowers.

My uncle when he was done planting his flowers turned to my dad and said," I am proud of you. Every day, you are my hero because you treat me like I am important. You see me and love me. I just want you to know I see you too."

With tears in his eyes, Dad replied," Thank you, I really needed to hear that."

My uncle then hugged my dad. It was on that day, I think I truly met my father for the first time. My dad, My Hero, My best friend."

Jimmy took a moment to wipe a tear from his eye.

He left his classmates and Bruce speechless.

Swallowing a lump in his throat, Carlos said," Man, Jimmy. I have a new respect for your Mom , you and all that served."

Bruce spoke next." Jimmy, you should think about writing a book. I bet your dad's story would help many."

Jimmy replied," Sharing my dad's story has helped me to realize my dreams. I want to be a counselor. I want to help people. But I also want to keep some of my dad to myself. I don't think I am ready to share him with the world."

Alice spoke then saying." I am with you Jimmy. There are just some memories to personal to share with the world."

Bruce glanced down at his watch." Oh, sorry gang, but class is dismissed. We will pick this up in the am."

Bruce grabbed his briefcase. He dashed out the door. Leaving his students to wonder why he was in such a hurry.

Leon had to stop and look at a map. He knew his father's address from 15 years ago, but would his father still be living there? And if he was, would his father even let him in?

Leon nervously walked in the direction of the large apartment complex that his father once lived in. It had been years since Leon stood in his father's shadow.

Painful memories ripped apart Leon's heart as he recalled the last time him saw his father.

Leon was a H.S. student then. Leon had just made honor roll. Leon's dad Jacob was supposed to see Leon that weekend.

Leon was super-excited to see his dad. Even through it was only going to be for two hours. Leon wanted to tell his dad he made honor roll, and the football team and about a girl he liked.

Jacob showed up for the visit, drunk and high. The exact reason why Leon's parents were no longer together. The exact reason why Leon only got to see his father every so often.

Not only was Jacob drunk and high, but he told Leon he was getting re-married. He told Leon he didn't have room for him in his life anymore and that Leon should just move on. Leon never saw his father again.

Leon suddenly felt sick to his stomach, as ghosts of his past haunted him. He made a quick run to a public restroom, and just in time too.

As Leon looked in the mirror after he washed his face, He repeated to himself," Pull it together man. You are here to help Frances."

Leon calmed himself down a bit before he started towards his father's last known address.

The projects where his father had once lived, had not changed. The buildings still looked rundown and lifeless. Even in the daytime it was a dangerous place to be in.

There were hookers and dealers hanging out on the steps leading up to the building.

There was children playing with broken toys because their welfare assisted mothers could not afford to buy new ones. One little boy had snot coming out of his nose. His mother was ten yards away from him using a crack pipe paying no mind to the tot.

No one answered when Leon knocked on the apartment door marked seven.

An old black woman opened up her apartment door just a crack to ask Leon," Baby, who are you looking for making all that noise?"

"Jacob Rivers." Leon replied.

"Oh, you mean Pastor Rivers his down at the mission down the block. He hasn't lived here in years." The woman said.

"Wait, you mean Jacob Rivers is a pastor?" Leon asked confused.

"Oh, Lordy, Lordy you are his son aren't you? That man has been trying to find you for years." The woman replied.

Leon's eyes went wide with disbelief. "Where can I find him?" Leon asked again.

"Boy, you can find him down the street. At the homeless mission." A crack dealer said.

Leon's mind could not wrap around the idea that his father was a minister. But when he saw it with his own eyes, he couldn't deny it.

His father stood in the middle of a group of homeless people passing out sandwiches and sharing God's word.

When Leon's eyes connected with his father's there were no words to describe how Leon felt in his heart.

All of Leon's anger, unforgiveness, darkness and sadness vanished into thin air and was replaced with only love.

Leon pushed his way into the crowd and right into his father's arms. Both men wept like babies.

Finally Jacob said," Everyone I am proud to introduce you to my son Leon."

In the quiet moments following the reunion Leon told his father why he was there.

Somehow in the fog of Leon's past, Leon recalled that his father once worked as a cleaner for a company called " Red Hot." A company owned by Frances' parents.

Memories were trigged as Leon recalled stories that his father had told him about the awful owners.

"Dad, do you recall when you worked for them?" Leon asked.

"Son, I might have been a raging drunk but I can recall everything about them. I even recall the fear I felt for that little girl. I even wrote to the child welfare about them. That's why I was fired."

"Dad, you wouldn't happen to have a copy of that letter would you?" Leon asked.

"No son. But wait a moment, I might have a copy of the letter they wrote to me in the storage unit." Jacob replied.

"Dad if you could find that letter it could give Frances a fighting chance." Leon replied.

"Why, don't you help me finish up here? Then we can go look in the shed, if I got any reply at all that's where it will be." Jacob said.

"Sure, Dad. What can I help you with?" Leon asked.

Jacob directed Leon to pass out bottled water.

Two hours later, father and son had gone through half the boxes in the unit. It was then Leon found a box with his name on it.

"What's this dad?" Leon asked.

Jacob turned to face Leon. Jacob's eyes became all misty and red. "Oh son, Don't think I didn't love you and try to find you. I wrote to your mother over the years and she didn't reply. When I did actually locate you, you were doing so good in your life that I didn't want to intrude on it. So my boy, I started collecting newspaper clippings and things about you."

Leon opened the box. The first thing Leon pulled out of the box was his first teddy bear.

"You still have this dad?" Leon asked surprised.

"Your mother got that teddy bear for you. She was a month clean and sober then. When she saw your little face light up she promised to never touch drugs again. I promised the same. And even though we were not stronger than our addictions, we were very much in love with our little boy."

"I just wish I would have gotten to know her and you. I wanted to have my parents so badly." Leon let a tear slip from his eye.

Leon then pulled out a diary.

"Well, maybe now you can son. You are holding the diary your mama kept when she was pregnant with you." Jacob revealed.

"I like that dad. I really would. If we are going to locate the letter, we better get back to work." Leon said slapping his father on the back.

When Bruce saw Sara running towards him crying, his heart stopped.

Sara fell into his arms. "It can't be true. It just can't be."

Bruce lowered Sara into a chair gently. He then knelt in front of her. Taking her hands.

Sara was shaking.

"Easy now. Take a few deep breaths, slowly now, in and out." Bruce said.

Sara struggled to calm down but finally did.

"What's this all about Sara?" Bruce asked.

"I just came from seeing Frances. She told me that Jimmy is the father. She said Carlos and Leon drugged them." Sara replied.

"When? How?" Bruce deiced it would be best to act surprised.

"She said, well, the old man and teenager said that it happened at a coffee shop. That it was an accident." Sara replied in between sobs.

"We don't know if any of this is true. We have to keep calm. We have to talk to Carlos." Bruce said.

"If Carlos did, I don't think he will admit to it." Sara replied.

"I think the only thing we can do then is wait until the baby is born and do a D and A test."Bruce said.

"Do you really think that is best?" Sara asked.

"I do." Bruce replied.

Then a lightbulb went off in Sara's head. "You knew didn't you? That's why you were jumpy the last time I saw you. How can you not tell me? I thought we were friends!" Sara screamed.

"Sara, please calm down. I can't deny it. Frances told me. But I didn't know if I could believe her. Them, I didn't know if I could believe them." Bruce said.

"Don't you dare tell me to calm down? How could you keep a secret like that from me? "Sara was crying hard now.

"I am sorry. I am so sorry." Bruce said.

Sara let out a loud wail. "What am I going to do Bruce? I am all alone in the world. How can I raise a grandchild, a sick adopted daughter and Jimmy all on my own?"

"Oh Sara, you are not alone. God is with you always. And if you let me, I like to help." Bruce handing Sara a tissue said.

"What? You're hitting on me now? God Bruce!" Sara stormed out of the café then.

"Freedom- Chapter ten"

"Carlos, you are awful quiet today. Are you ok?" Buck said.

Carlos, who was changing oil on a car replied," I am just thinking about class today. There is a guy in the class named Jimmy. I pretty much have been awful to him. There was something I did, something terrible. He has been sharing this amazing story about his Dad he came home from Nam, a changed man. Jimmy really touched my heart today man. I have been thinking about, well that thing I did to him and well I just don't know how to make it right."

"You know, I was in Nam too." Buck said.

"You were?" Carlos asked surprised.

"Why don't I tell you about it during lunch?" Buck said.

At lunch time, Carlos and Buck split a tuna salad and some coffee.

Buck started to tell Carlos about Nam.

"I was a young man when I entered Nam. Totally naïve. But when I came back I was a changed man. I knew more about the world then I ever cared to know. I was a prisoner of war. So was my best friend. My best friend saved my hive more times I could count. When we came back, we were really messed up. I mean I lost my mind boy. My best friend was the only one that could reach me. When I finally recovered another tragic event happened in my life."

"What happened Buck?" Carlos asked, his voice filed with compassion.

"Ah, yeah about that my real name is not Buck. It's Frenchie. When I came back from the war, I changed it because my old self was gone and well I only had a buck in my pocket when I came back." Frenchie replied.

"Wait a moment! Was your best friend named Simon?" Carlos asked excited.

"Yes." Frenchie replied asking, "How do you know about Simon."

"I am in Collage with Simon's son Jimmy. His mom Sara has been helping Frances!" Carlos replied.

"You wouldn't fool an old man would you?" Frenchie asked.

"No sir." Carlos replied.

"Please, I need to see them! Will you take me to them?" Frenchie asked.

"Sure come on." Carlos replied.

Jacob and Leon spent the entire night looking for the letter. They went through every box, every drawer, and every nook and couldn't find it.

"I am so sorry son. I would have thought it would be here. I am so sorry." Jacob said. "There is no other place it could be?" Leon asked disappointed.

"No, I don't think so." Jacob said sadly. "Maybe I could come back with you and testify on Frances behalf."

"I don't mean to be respectful but with your history it might do more harm than good." Leon said.

"Maybe you are right son." Jacob replied.

"I really wish we could find that letter." Leon replied. "I know son. Do you want me to go back with you for moral support?" Jacob asked. "That would be nice, but I would feel selfish taking you away from your important work... Those people need you." Leon replied.

"Son, you don't have to spare my feelings. I understand you are going to have to get used to me having you in my life again." Jacob replied.

"Dad, I don't know what to say but thank you." Leon said hugging his father.

After a wonderful, tearful and surprising reunion between Jimmy, Sara and Frenchie that night before, Frenchie came to class with Jimmy.

As Jimmy stood up to address his classmates, Frenchie smiled. "Everyone, I like you to meet my father's best friend Frenchie." Jimmy said.

Frenchie stood at the thundering applause.

Leon who had just returned just a few moments before, shot Carlos a ' What-in-the-world-is –going- on look.' Carlos shot a look back that said," I will tell you later."

"Before, we get started Jimmy, I like to hear from Leon as to where he ran off to." Bruce said.

Jimmy said," I am sure we would all like to know that."

Leon filled everyone in on what was happening. Bruce and Leon's classmates were filled with questions, but those questions would have to wait until after class.

Jimmy said," I know I have been telling you about my dad, but I think Frenchie should take it from here…. Frenchie…."

Frenchie slowly addressed the class from a chair. "Some stories don't always have happy endings kids. I am sorry to say. Just when everyone thought I was getting better, my world fell apart again. I found out both of my kidneys were failing. I would need a new kidney to live. I had been poisoned in the war. The VA gave me little hope. They said I was a walking dead man.

It was the fourth of July when I broke the news to Simon. He had come to the VA hospital to visit me.

IT was our little tradition Simon and I would have a picnic lunch. Anyway Simon knew something was laying heavy on my heart. He kept asking me what was wrong.

So as the fireworks lit up the sky, I poured my heart out to my best friend, ,y only friend.

When I was done. Simon turned to me and said, "Hell brother, I Have two kidneys and I only need one. So take one of mine."

Just like that. Like he was lending me a light or something. That very night Simon got tested to see if he was a match."

"What happened?" Bruce asked.

"Well, on the way home from the VA. Simon saw a man beating his wife. Simon stopped his car to intervene. When the man saw Simon coming to help the woman, he shot Simon twice. Once in the head and once in that chest. Simon was brain dead by the time they got him back to the VA.

When I heard the news the next day, I had another mental break down."

Jimmy spoke up then. "Not all stories have a happy ending, but all the stories God creates does. Tell them what happened next Frenchie."

"You see kids, It was Simon who saved my life, because he was an organ donator. I got his kidney."

"I never believed in miracles until I realized the friendship my best friend gave me was a miracle." Frenchie said as tears rolled down his wrinkled face.

Carlos said, "That's a beautiful testament to God's love for all of us. Maya Angelou said it best however," And when great souls die, after a period piece blooms, slowly and always irregularly. Spaces fill with a kind of soothing electric vibration. Our senses, restored, never to be the same, whisper to us. They existed. They existed. We can be. Be and be better. For they existed."

The class feel silent then. The souls took in the peace and quiet of that wondrous moment.

With a liver-spotted covered hand Frenchie said," As much as I loved Simon, he didn't save my life God did. It's not unreachable - it's not unreasonable - it's just what we are here to do. To become the best version of ourselves as Spirit and then share our wisdom and love with all others. We don't require training, or a certificate, we can just start right away - if we choose to.

Your life is a sacred journey. And it is about change, growth, discovery, movement, transformation, continuously expanding your vision of what is possible, stretching your soul, learning to see clearly and deeply, listening to your intuition, taking courageous challenges at every step along the way. You are on the path... exactly where you are meant to be right now... And from here, you can only go forward, shaping your life story into a magnificent tale of triumph, of healing, of courage, of beauty, of wisdom, of power, of dignity, and of love."

The class gave both Jimmy and Frenchie a round of gratitude.

By Lunch, Leon had reviled to Sara, Bruce and his classmates what had happened. Everyone was hopeful that Jacob may find the letter.

But their hopes were soon dashed. Sara reviled to everyone that the DA had more damning evidence against Frances.

"A safety deposit box was found that Frances had paid for. In it there was a list of who Frances would kill, how she would do it and why." Sara shared.

Three weeks later, the jury was selected and the trial had begun.

Frances was starting to show signs of cracking, even though Sara and Dr. Turner tried to help her.

Things were not going well for Frances at all. Frances 'parents had taken the stand denying that they had abused her. People were coming to testify on Frances' violent behavior.

There were classmates she had beat up, bullied and paid off.

There was her former nanny that said Frances had once chased her with a knife.

The press and Jury all seemed to be taking the DA's side.

"Carlos you are very quiet today. Is everything all right?" Frenchie asked.

Carlos broke down then sharing what he had done to Frances and Jimmy.

Without judgment, Frenchie listened. "You have to tell Sara." Frenchie said.

"How?" Carlos asked." Will you be there when I tell her please?"

"Of course I will." Frenchie promised.

Leon at that same moment was pouring his heart out to Fr. Miller. "I told Carlos, not to do it. But I just stood by and watched laughing as he put it into Jimmy's drink. I don't know how to make it right now."

Fr. Miller picked at a loose thread on his pants." Do you want forgiveness?"

"Father, every night I drop to my knees to beg God to forgive me. I know he has but I don't know if I can forgive myself. I mean for years, I judged my father but look at me." Leon admitted.

"Son, you have to talk to Jimmy. You have to tell him you and Carlos made a mistake. The good book says, "Love does not keep a record of wrongs. Your friend Jimmy loves you and will forgive you. You have always had all the wisdom and the love of the Universe within your heart. The moment you choose to open the door to your heart, you will discover who you are: a Divine Being, a pure Human Angel. You will be able to draw from the sacred source of your heart, testifying to the Truth of the God and unconditionally loving the whole world as a reflection of the unconditional love that you feel for yourself. For God lives in you. As, he lives in all men. Then it will become natural to fully express your nature as a Human Angel. Then it will become natural to put your life in service to others. This does not mean renunciation and sacrifice, but the miraculous abundance of all of the goods of God." The kind old Priest said.

"I don't know father. If I were Jimmy I wouldn't let Carlos and I off the hook so easy." Leon said.

"Have you talked to your dad about this?" Father Miller asked in a low and gentle tone.

"I was planning on calling him tonight. But that's another thing. How do I talk to my dad about this when he has been out of my life for more than 15 years? It's not like we can pick up where we left off. My dad is so different now. He's changed and so have I."

The old priest with the kind heart shared this story with young and confused Leon." Jesus shares it with his disciples, the Pharisees and others. In the story, a father has two sons. The younger son asks for his inheritance before the father dies, and the father agrees. The younger son, after wasting his fortune (the word "prodigal" means "wastefully extravagant"), goes hungry during a famine, and becomes so destitute he longs to eat the same food given to hogs, unclean animals in Jewish culture. He then returns home with the intention of repenting and begging his father to be made one of his hired servants, expecting his relationship with his father is likely severed. Regardless, the father finds him on the road and immediately welcomes him back as his son and holds a feast to celebrate his return, which includes killing a fattened calf usually reserved for special occasions. The older son refuses to participate, stating that in all the time he has worked for the father, he never disobeyed him; yet, he did not even receive a goat to celebrate with his friends. The father reminds the older son that the son has always been with him and everything the father has belongs to the older son (his inheritance). But, they should still celebrate the return of the younger son because he was lost and is now found. You see son, your father was lost in sin, dead in the darkness of evil and now he has returned to you. You should not fear his return into your life but rejoice and embrace it."

"Thanks Father. Talking to you really helped a lot." Leon said before leaving the church.

Jacob could not believe his eyes! He went into his shed to chase a mouse out of it, when he did he found the letter !

He ran upstairs ,grabbed his cell phone and booked a flight to New Milford.

Two hours later, Jacob was sitting in a window seat on a Southwest flight headed to see his son.

"Bruce, I feel hapless. I don't think I can win Frances case. The cards are stacked against her. Even with Dr. Turner's testimony." Sara spilled her guts to the one man she knew would listen.

Bruce and Sara had started dating right before the trail began but they had been keeping it a secret from everyone. "We can't give up. God is with us honey." Bruce replied.

"Bruce, we have to be realistic. The evidence against Frances is damming. We have to figure out what to do with the baby if she is convicted. If Jimmy is the father, he is not ready to be one, and I can't raise a baby alone at my age. I am over 50." Sara let out a deep long breath then.

"Sara, we can be a family. We can adopt Frances and the baby. We can raise the baby as our own." Bruce suggested.

Pulling a ring from his pocket, Bruce said," I love you Sara. I want us to get married."

Sara's eyes filled with tears." Oh Bruce, I do love you, but I don't think this will solve our issues. I mean what will Jimmy think? What will the baby do when he/she finds out his/her mother is really grandma? I am crazy about you Bruce but-"

Bruce kissed Sara before she could finish speaking. "It might be crazy but I am only doing what my heart is telling me to do. I am asking you to marry me Sara. Marry me because I love you. Marry me because I never thought my heart would beat again until I met you."

Sara blinked hard. Her face became flushed." I think I need some water." Sara said.

Bruce reached for her hand." Sara, you know we are meant to be together. Why is it so hard for you to say "Yes?" Is it because you are still in love with Simon?"

"Bruce, I'll always be in love with Simon. You have to understand that. He is a part of my soul. When I look at Jimmy, I see him. To tell you the truth sometimes late at night, when I only have my thoughts to keep me company, I can still feel his touch. I don't want to hurt you Bruce. I don't but I don't want to lie to you either."

"So , are you telling me that when I touch you, and when I kiss you, you don't feel anything?" Bruce heartbroken asked.

"No, Bruce. I am saying that it scares the hell out of me because you are now part of my soul too. If I lost you like I lost Simon, I wouldn't be able to go on." Sara's gaze dropped to the floor then.

"Baby, say "Yes." You are not going to lose me. I am not going anywhere." Bruce replied, as he gently lifted Sara face to meet his gaze.

"Before I say "yes," we will have to talk to Jimmy. We have to tell him everything. I can't marry you without his blessing Bruce." Sara said.

"You drive a hard bargain. But I will do anything to make you my wife." Bruce replied.

"You did what?" Jimmy screamed as he pushed Carlos.

"Let, it out Jimbo. I derive it. I was a real jerk. I know." Carlos replied.

Jimmy balled up his hands into tight fists. He raced towards Carlos, he wanted to punch him, but hit the wall instead.

"I am out of here!" Jimmy stormed out of Frenchie's office.

Frenchie went after Jimmy. "Jimmy, wait! Please let's talk." Frenchie called after him.

Jimmy turned around. "Talk about what!!!!!!!! About how that low-life ruined not only my life but Frances? Or maybe how my mom is going to have a heart-attack when she hears about this! And how is Alice going to feel? And what about that poor baby! I am not ready to be a father and Frances can't be a mother! Leave me alone Frenchie please!"

"Jimmy, he made a mistake. He feels horrible." Frenchie replied.

"He feels horrible! What about how I feel!" Jimmy yelled.

Carlos stepped out of the office then. "You feel betrayed, hurt, used…. That's how I felt when I did that to you. To tell you the truth I felt jealous too."

"Wait! What??? Why???' Jimmy asked.

"Jimmy, You and Alice. That's why I did it. You have a tight bond with Alice I'll never have, you share your childhood. You rescued her from her mother more times than I ever will. I was jealous of that." Carlos admitted.

"But Carlos, you have Alice's heart. Something I will never have." Jimmy said.

"Do I? I mean lately you are the one that makes her laugh, that makes her smile. "Carlos replied.

"Oh Carlos, she loves you man. She loves you the way my dad loved my mom. I might make her laugh but you make her entire soul shine with joy." Jimmy said.

"I am so sorry Jimmy. You have to forgive me. Please forgive me. Please ... "Carlos clung to Jimmy crying.

"I need to go for a walk. You two don't follow me." Jimmy ordered.

Carlos and Frenchie gave Jimmy the space he wanted.

Sara and Bruce were startled when they ran into Leon on the sidewalk outside the café.

Breathless, Leon said," I need to talk to both of you."

"Why don't we go back to my office?" Bruce suggested.

The trio walked the short mile back to Bruce's office.

Leon, Bruce and Sara sat down. "What's on your mind Leon?" Bruce asked.

Leon shifted in his seat. "Carlos and I have done something awful. Something we will regret forever. Jimmy is the father of Frances' baby."

Sara's heart sunk as the words poured out of Leon's mouth.

"Oh, My God! I feel like I am going to pass out. Bruce can you get me some water please." Sara asked.

Bruce poured Sara a glass of water.

"Miss. Winter are you all right?" Leon asked.

"Let me just get my bearings son. Then we will talk." Sara replied.

Alice pulled out her cell-phone from a blue purse. She dialed Carlos' work number. Frenchie answered the phone on the second ring.

"Hi, it's Alice. May I please speak with Carlos?" Alice asked.

"Yes, sure hold on." Frenchie replied.

Hopeful, Carlos asked," Is that Jimmy?" "No Alice." Frenchie replied.

At the sound of his wife's voice, the knot in Carlos' stomach grew even tighter.

"What the heck is going on Carlos? Jimmy just ran into me. He was very upset. He said I married the devil. That he was the father of Frances' baby. I want you home now mister, I want answers!"

Frenchie saw by the look on Carlos' face that he was in the dog house. So he let Carlos take the rest of the day off.

"Go talk to Alice. I will stay here in case Jimmy comes back." Frenchie replied.

"Why would you do that to my son? He has done nothing but be a friend to you!" Sara said with her hands on her hips.

Leon searched his heart, looking for a way to explain. "It's so hard to explain this, but we did it out of jealousy. Jimmy had everything we wanted. A loving father, adoring mother, a stable home, smarts, good-looks. We were angry and jealous. We were lost, we felt unloved. We will never forgive ourselves."

Sara's heart melted then." Leon, don't you know God loves all his kids? You are so loved that Jesus would have hung on the cross, even if you were the only person on Earth."

"You have to understand, I barely had enough pieces of a parent to make a whole one. I figured if my parents couldn't love me, no one would." Leon cried.

Sara open her arms. Leon feel into them.

"We are going to figure this out son. I promise." Sara said. Bruce reassured them both.

The handprint that Alice left on Carlos' face after slapping him burned.

Alice started crying." I am sorry, Carlos."

Carlos took Alice into his loving arms." It's ok sweetheart. I did something horrible. I am the one that needs to repent!"

Gasping for breath, Alice asked," Why Carlos why did you do it?"

Carlos looked deep into his wife's eyes. Eyes that mirrored pain and confusion.

"I was so full of hate. Hate because my mother is so sick. Hate because I felt lost. Hate because my grandpa disowned us. Hate because I couldn't be the husband you derived. Hate because I thought I was going to lose you to Jimmy." Carlos admitted.

"Oh, Carlos you are everything I ever wanted in a husband and everything I could want. We have to make things right for Jimmy and Frances." Alice said.

"I know." Carlos humbly replied.

Sara, Jimmy and Bruce sat down for a long heart to heart talk. Tearful and emotional, Sara said," Bruce and I know what Carlos and Leon did to you and Frances."

Jimmy was shocked. "How? How did you know? I never told a soul."

"Well, not only did Carlos and Leon admit it to us, but Frances was semi-aware. Well not Frances but her other personalities were." Sara replied.

"Oh." Jimmy said squirming in his seat. "I don't know what to do mom. I mean, Naturally the right thing to do would be for me to marry Frances. But I don't think I can handle the responsibility. I don't want to abandon Frances and the baby either."

"Son, Bruce and I have been dating for a while now. I didn't know how to tell you so I was going to wait until after the trial. Bruce proposed to me. But I told him I can only marry him with your blessing." Sara reviled.

Jimmy turned to Bruce asking," Do you love my mom?"

"Yes, very much." Bruce replied.

"Mom, do you love Bruce?" Jimmy then asked Sara.

"Yes, son I do. But Bruce knows that your happiness comes before my own. I would never do anything to hurt you." Sara replied.

Jimmy smiled wide then." Well, I got news for you. I love you both. If getting married makes you both happy then you have my blessing."

Bruce shook Jimmy's hand. Sara kissed her son." Oh, Jimmy, you are just like your father." Sara said with tears in her eyes.

Bruce then slipped the engagement ring onto Sara's hand.

"We want to adopt the baby son. You and

Frances have your whole lives ahead of you." Bruce said.

"No. I can't let you do that. This may not be the way I planned to become a father, but it's my child. I want to raise him/her with your help of course. I want to be the father my dad was. If that means living my life not the way I exactly planned so be it. After all as Frenchie says," "Not all stories have a happy ending, but all the stories God creates does" Jimmy said.

"Jimmy, you are going to be a great dad. Just like your father." Sara kissed her son on the forehead just like she did when he was a little boy.

"But what about Frances mom? I mean I just can't have full custody of the child." Jimmy asked.

"Given Frances illness, yes you can." Sara replied.

Jacob was desperate to find his son. He had searched the campus, doom and the local coffee bars.

As Jacob was heading back to the Campus, he bumped right into Leon.

"Dad, what are you doing here?" Leon asked surprised.

"Son, are you all-right? You look like you have been crying." Jacob said.

"I am. I just told my friend's mother about what Carlos and I did. Can we talk about that later? What are you doing here?" Leon asked again.

Jacob pulled a piece of paper out of his pocket. Jacob and Leon sat on a bench. Jacob handed his son the paper.

Leon read the following," Dear, Mr. Jacob, All-through, your concern for your bosses daughter is Nobel without solid proof that she is being abused, we can't investigate anymore. We will however keep your letter on file.

Thank you,

Dept. Of Child Welfare"

"Dad, I am really glad you found this letter, but I don't see how it will help Frances. It says right in the letter no child abuse was found." Leon replied.

"Son, "Not all stories have a happy ending, but all the stories God creates does. On the plane I sat next to a woman who for some reason seemed to me like she knew me. We got to talking. Son, she was the social worker that investigated Frances case so many years ago. Son, she told me Frances case haunted her for many years. She told me all the disgusting details. She is at a hotel right here in town she wants to testify for Frances!" Jacob said.

"We have to find Miss. Winter and tell her." Leon said.

The following morning the jury, judge, newspaper reporters, DA and Frances' friends all wept at the story that social worker told.

"For years, the face of a scared little girl haunted me. The face that belonged to Frances. The first time I met Frances, she was four years old. She was lying in a hospital bed holding a stuffed dog. She had a leg that was broken in three spots. The E.R doctor and my gut told me that Frances was a victim of child abuse. I filed serval reports on Frances' behalf. Each time for some reason, my boss tossed it aside. Making excuses for the parents. I came to understand my boss was getting paid off by Frances parents. So I tried to take matters into my own hands. I took pictures of the dirty house that poor baby lived in. I interviewed her pre-school teacher who also confirmed the abuse. Together we set out to save Frances.

We worked for two years, collecting pictures, witness testimony and proof. We were going to turn it into the DA.

On the way to the DA'S office, my breaks went out on my car. They had been cut! I woke up three days later in a hospital bed.

The teacher, had skipped town because her life had been threated. I dropped the case for fear that my children might get hurt next."

Sara stood in front of the Judge, As she was about to rest her case the DA said," Your honor, may I approach the bench."

The judge replied," Yes you may."

The court room became very still and silent. No one dared to even shift in their seats. As The DA said," In light of this new witness's testimony, I like to drop all charges. The defendant's lawyer was right all along. This girl needs a hospital not a jail."

The judge agreed. The judge announced to the courtroom that the case was dismissed. Those who knew and loved Frances were pleased with the judge's ruling. But outside the courtroom things were a bit different.

Many people protested Frances' release for fear of her metal state. They spit and tried to grab at Frances as Sara and Dr. Turner raced to get her to the safety of Dr. Turner's car.

Outside the courthouse, Carlos and Jimmy also ran into one another.

"Hey." Carlos said in a low and rumbling tone." Great news about Frances, isn't it."

Jimmy replied," Yes."

Shifting his weight from one foot to another, Carlos asked," Do you think we can talk?"

"I think, we need too. But not here. Too many eyes." Jimmy said referring to the reporters.

"How about we go somewhere for coffee?" Carlos replied. "Um, why don't we make it tea?" Jimmy replied giving Carlos a half-cocked smile.

At a local diner, the two Collage Seniors hashed things out.

"Do you hate me?" Carlos asked frankly.

Dipping his tea bag into hot water, Jimmy replied," I should but I don't. I went home and thought about things last night. I am going to raise the baby. I am still hurt and confused but not with you. I feel hurt Carlos, that you were in so much pain, You and Leon that you felt the need to do that to me. Yes, I was in love with Alice once. A long time ago, but that was a lifetime ago. I can see now that you and Alice are soulmates. I would never do anything to tear you apart. Never! I care about you two way too much. I want to forgive you Carlos. I think that was the old Carlos that did that to me, not the Carlos I know now." Jimmy said.

"I take full responsibility. You know you are right, I was another Carlos then. I pray every single night, for that Carlos not to return."

Jimmy sighed then. "When we accept Christ, we are all new creatures."

"It really is like Frenchie said," Not all stories have a happy ending, but all the stories God creates does." Carlos replied.

Jimmy held out his hand." Friends??"

Carlos shook his head no." No brothers." Carlos said, shaking Jimmy's hand.

"I like that. Brothers." Jimmy replied.

Alice popped into the diner then. She had been following her husband and Jimmy since they left the courthouse." Everything all right boys?" She asked concerned.

"Yes, My brother and I were just thinking up baby names." Jimmy smiled. Alice hugged Jimmy and then Carlos." Oh you don't know how happy I am to hear that." Alice said.

"Baby, Bottles and Life- Chapter eleven "

Months after the trail, Frances give birth to a healthy baby boy, that Jimmy named Simon.

Bruce and Sara got married on a snowy afternoon in Father Miller's church. Family and Friends witnessed the blessed event.

Weeks after Bruce and Sara got married, Jimmy asked Frances to marry him. Even though he knew Frances could never love him as a wife, he wanted to do the right thing for her and his child.

Frances agreed. Then changed her mind. Then agreed again.

Carlos ended up being Jimmy's best man. Jimmy forgive Carlos and Leon for what they had done. Jimmy thinks Frances did as well.

After getting married by the Justice of the Peace, Jimmy and Frances moved into a mother /daughter home with Sara and Bruce.

Frances saw a doctor regularly. Slowly she began to get better, so much so she got a part-time job at a factory . She did as much as she was able to help raise her son.

Jimmy graduated Collage with honors. He went on to become a counselor. He was a great dad, just like Simon.

Frenchie retired. Carlos took over the gas station. He was very successful.

With her new treatment, Carlos' mother was stable enough to be released from the hospital. She moved into a group home. She was very happy there.

Alice, became a reporter for a local paper. After graduation she held a intervention for her mother, but it failed. Her mother passed away, just a year after Alice and Carlos delivered their first child Frances. A bouncing baby girl who loved her godmother and auntie Frances.

Leon and Jacob found their way back into each other's levies. After graduating, Leon became a Minster also. He ran the homeless shelter with his dad.

Sara and Bruce adored Simon. They lavished him with love. Bruce retired from teaching.

The last class he ever taught was the one Jimmy was in.

Sara, well Sara went on to write a book about her time as Frances' lawyer. She donates the profits to help those with Mental illness.

Alan, Jimmy's uncle feel head over heels in love with Carlos' mom. Sara allowed Alan to move into the same group home as her, so they could be together. They are currently planning their wedding.

Sarah, Turner and Fr. Miller, the three angels sent to earth to help , returned to Heaven for their next mission.

As they entered the pearly gates, they heard a booming voice say," Welcome home my good and faithful servants."

The three angels beamed in God's love light.

And I Simon, grandson of Simon, son of Jimmy and Frances learned that," Everything you are seeking is found in Love. Be soft. Do not let the world make you hard. Do not let pain make you hate. Do not let the bitterness steal your sweetness. Take pride that even though the rest of the world may disagree with you, you still believe it to be a beautiful place and believe in you.....be strong, but not rude; be kind, but not weak; be bold, but not a bully; be thoughtful, but not lazy; be humble, but not timid; be proud but not arrogant; have humor, but without folly." Before you speak, listen. Before you write, think. Before you spend, earn. Before you invest, seek knowledge. Before you criticize, wait. Before you pray, forgive. Before you quit, try. Before you destroy, build and before you leave this earth.....Make a difference! You never know how brave you are until you love those who don't love you back, Pray for those who have hurt you, and find beauty in what the world the world calls ugly. Being true is the best way to let others see your inner Godlike beauty and to inspire their search for their own Divine spark. As a Christian just remember to take care of God's sheep because God will take care of the wolves. There is no righteousness in suffering; no merit in martyrdom. The denial of Love and deprivation of pleasure gain us nothing yet cost everything. You see, when we reject our good, we disinherit ourselves from our Divine birthright; effortless abundance, perfect peace, and ebullient joy. In this moment, stand firm in your heart; boldly claim what is yours: the unconditional, eternal Love of God."

WHERE TO SEEK HELP IF YOU OR SOMEONE
IS SUFFERING WITH A MENTAL ILLNESS.

In Crisis?

Call 1-800-273-TALK

Questions for book clubs

1. Have you ever known someone with a mental illness?
2. If so how did you help them?
3. Did you ever avoid spending time with someone because they were mentally ill?
4. How do you think society can help those with a mental illness?
5. Do you feel that most mass shooters are affected by mental illness?
6. If you fear those who have a mental illness, what can you do to overcome the fear?
7. How can we teach our children about mental illness?

8. Do you feel that bullying contributes to mental illness?

Questions to ask your doctor about Mental health....

What does it mean to have a mental illness?

What is considered a serious mental illness?

What causes mental illness?

Is anyone immune to mental illness?

Can mental illness be prevented?

Once someone has had a mental illness can they ever get better again?

How common is mental illness?

What are some of the warning signs of mental illness?

What should I do if I know someone who appears to have all of the symptoms of a serious mental disorder?

What is the difference between mental health professionals?

How can I find a mental health professional right for my child or myself?

What treatment options are available?

If I become involved in treatment what do I need to know?

What do I need to know about medications?

If a medication is prescribed to me and I begin to feel better after taking it is it okay to stop taking it?

How can I get help paying for my prescriptions?

Where can I go for help?

How do I find a local support group?

Notes:

Notes:

Notes:

Notes:

Notes:

Notes:

Notes: